Mourning Air

Leena Magdi

This edition was published by The Dreamwork Collective
The Dreamwork Collective LLC, Dubai, United Arab Emirates
thedreamworkcollective.com
Printed and bound in the United Arab Emirates
Cover and design: Nuno Moreira, NMDESIGN.ORG
Text © Leena Magdi, 2025
ISBN: 978-9948-715-35-1
Approved by National Media Council Dubai, United Arab Emirates
MC-02-01-6233937

All rights reserved. No part of this publication may be reproduced, stored, or transmitted in any form or by any means, electronic, mechanical, photocopying, recording, or otherwise, without prior permission of the publishers. The right of Leena Magdi to be identified as the author of this work has been asserted and protected under the UAE Copyright and Authorship Protection Law No. 7.

Mourning Air

Leena Magdi

A MEMOIR OF
SUDDEN LOSS

I'm with you always, Hamoodi
You're with me, all ways, habeebi
Depth over distance, my love
We will always be eternally near

INTRODUCTION

I grew up in the United States as a child of immigrants—an immigrant myself though I had no recollection of living in my home country. I went back to Sudan as an adult and lived as a foreign native: a familiar face in unfamiliar culture, surroundings, and semantics. The war came, and I became a refugee. I have always belonged in places I do not seemingly fit.

I was born in Sudan and moved to California when I was about five years old. I spent my life in the Bay Area. In 2013, at twenty-two years old, a fresh college graduate, I moved back to Sudan and stayed for two years. Life took me away and brought me back again in 2020, a few weeks shy of my twenty-ninth birthday. Those were the last few years I spent in Sudan. The last years with my brother.

The October 2021 military coup in Khartoum took place after the 2019 revolution and the peaceful transition of government. It was a violent betrayal of a nation. The war started two years later, in April 2023. My breaking was in the year between, in August 2022—the month that took my brother's life.

The recent horror unfolding in Sudan went largely unmarked by the world. There were no mass evacuations. The ones that did come, came far too late. In the early days of the war, media coverage was practically nonexistent. It was a news story as part of a news cycle that ended in a couple of weeks. It's been one and a half years since the war started. One year and a half, and the war is still ongoing. A country died. Over ten million people have been displaced. International silence. Such is the story for most African nations. Unrecognized and dismissed.

At my brother's funeral, three days after he was murdered, a well-meaning guest pulled me aside in an effort to offer advice or counsel me and said, *"I'm sorry, but a brother is not a son."* I knew she was concerned about my parents' well-being. What I wanted to tell her was that no one could be more concerned about my parents than my two sisters and me. I did not cry during the days of my brother's funeral. Neither did my sisters. We did not openly grieve. And though we did not discuss it, I know we were holding space for our parents. We did not need any direction to do so. I quickly realized that sibling grief is often unrecognized and dismissed.

My hope for this book is that it will paint a picture of a mind in grief.

I have seen some of grief's many faces that revealed grieving in different ways: different versions of myself, different homes, different people I love. Sometimes we leave our homes willingly. Sometimes we're made to leave; we're forced. Things are taken from us, stolen violently. In both cases, there is a grieving that happens. Sometimes death comes suddenly. People die young. People are murdered. Sometimes we know death is coming. It is anticipated. People grow old. People get sick. It doesn't soften the blow. It only changes the angle.

This is a book about accepting our grief. In whatever way it chooses to greet us. Welcoming it in our lungs. Learning to breathe with it. When we don't, we feel suffocated because grief needs to be shared. It needs to be witnessed.

The following pages are my relief. A written exhale. They are my breath work. I am of the conviction that we all have divine magic embedded within us. In this life, part of our purpose is to learn how to activate it.

In putting this together, I realized there were many floating pieces in my mind that played a part in helping me walk with grief. Most of them, like writing, happened without my conscious intention for healing. I've always loved writing and I've always written. Similarly, though I didn't start professionally practicing Positive Psychology until later in life, I realize it has always been a part of my life: My mother's deep love for spirituality that she imbedded in us. My father's tendency to look for the good, fiercely, something my brother inherited. Something he drilled in the rest of us. These things that I grew up with became a part of who I am, strengths I didn't notice or pay attention to. In positive psychology, we call things like this character strengths. There's a survey we do that lists out our top strengths, and I was pleasantly surprised to see just how aligned the results were with what I knew to be true about myself. More often than not, it is these small habits we build over time, the things we don't pay attention to, the small pieces of advice we don't remember giving, the mundane stuff, that come into play when the worst happens.

After loss, the air changes around us. It's heavier and lighter at the same time. It's like a veil is lifted. It seems impossible to keep going. It feels like we have to try to keep living. But we don't. We keep breathing, and we don't even notice it. The breath may seem heavier, but it's still there. Our strengths work the same way. Situations paralyze us, but our strengths keep working, and we don't have to notice. They are a gift inside every single person.

Character strengths are a classification of positive traits that reflect our core identity. Whereas the majority of personality tests tell us what we are good at, Character Strength assessments illuminate who we are. The top strengths are called signature strengths. Expressing and detailing my journey were explicitly and implicitly guided by each one of my signature strengths: honesty, spirituality, love of learning, perspective, and hope. When I look back on my life so far, I notice that each section of my journey is tied to a strength that I feel allowed me to excavate and embrace that part of myself. The reason I chose to frame each segment of the book in this way is because signature strengths are intrinsic to who we are; they exist within us whether we are aware of them or not. They work for us and with us.

You will see that I talk about synchrony in life. This is a personal realization that has helped me live in companionship with my grief as well as my joys. We often think of synchrony as two forces moving together with a common purpose, towards a common goal. To me, synchrony is good and bad existing in one moment—not that they *can* exist in *a* moment, but that they *do* exist in *every* moment. If we pause and study our moments, we will see that in every moment we have lived, not one has been contained in all good or all bad. Synchrony has encompassed them all. Time was designed that way. We were designed that way; our birth marks the starting point towards the day of our death. Synchrony is not to be confused with synchronicity—meaningful "coincidences"—which is also important to recognize and become aware of. Synchrony is pervasive and ubiquitous. I have come to realize that synchrony is a complex duality of opposite forces. They seemingly move with conflicting purposes and circumstance, yet stealthily and beautifully integrate into one moment, one person, one event. Even into the horrific. The secret to synchrony exists in the secret to breath: The exhale exists within the inhale.

Though everyone's process is different, I do believe grief is a lifelong companion, and my goal is to share the similarities that may resonate across tragedies: the confusion, anger, love, guilt, sporadic memories, hope, and all that exist in unique synchrony. For this reason, I have not structured this book in a linear timeline, as experiencing grief is not structured; it is as volatile as it is still.

This is not a story in the traditional sense of stories that have a clearly marked beginning, middle, and end. You will not find coherence here because grief is not coherent. Grief does not know logic. There is no beginning, middle, and end. It is all present still. That is the reality of grief. It is every day renewed. There is no climax but an unquestionable, continual catharsis.

This is my story of escaping a forgotten war. Mourning a forgotten country. And grieving as a forgotten mourner.

FIRST BREATH

Honesty

As I drive down Sixtieth Street, towards the intersection of Abdalla-Altayib, to drop my kids off at preschool in the morning, there's a strange calmness in the air, almost serene. The *matarees* (barricades) from the night before have been moved aside and now blend in with the regular mounds of garbage that decorate the streets. There are other cars on the road; some corner shops are open. The ladies who sell tea and coffee on each block are back at their usual locations, with a few people already seated on the makeshift metal chairs, waiting for their morning brew. The hustle and bustle of daily life is almost back to normal. *Almost.* Every morning, I almost forget what happens on this very street every night. But all it takes is a simple turn of the head to the side of the road to jolt me back to reality. There, lined up on the sides of the road like stacks of dominoes, are the armed militias in their trucks, automatic rifles aimed and ready. Just sitting there, waiting, watching, preying. How can a space hold peace and terror simultaneously, in synchrony, all in the same moment?

I think back to joyful moments. Midnight on my thirtieth birthday, celebrating with my siblings, my sons and two nephews. Dancing in a hotel room, so happy that we're all together in one place, while being unable to forget the unpleasant circumstance that brought us together—my mother's recent diagnosis of a rare autoimmune disease. There, too, was synchrony.

I realize that I can be dressed in layers of hurt and still carry pockets of laughter. I can flow in rivers of happiness and still feel the ripples of stones. I do not have to be one or the other. Most days, I am both. That is the beauty of being, it is all-encompassing.

* * *

We are uniquely whole all the time. We have been taught to believe that there is a space between our good places and our bad places. Our war and our peace. But I don't believe that is the case. We are always both states in their entirety. In unique synchrony. We are constantly living this duality, for every day alive is a day closer to death. And yet it is still a blessing, a gift. So we say that we make the most of it. But we don't. Unless something tragic happens. Something that reminds us we won't be here forever. I learned at a young age that a disarming smile does not always mean a safe space, that these things can come together: Strength accompanying hardship. Forgiveness in the absence of resolution. As I grew, I realized most of our lives are lived in these areas. My own identity doesn't fit so snug in its original riverbed. It flows between Golden Gate straits and intersections of Blue and White, carrying waves and streams together.

Very few things are as clear as day and night.

* * *

The difference between pain and peace isn't a lack of hurt; it's that peace isn't selfish enough to demand your attention. Peace patiently waits until you are ready to see, appreciate, and choose her. Knowing that she comes hand in hand with pain. Peace is your willingness to see her through it, still.

* * *

There's meaning in everything. Everywhere. All around us. We just have to be open enough to receive it. Our story is always being written. Every moment we have is another moment to see the peace and beauty around us. There is always ugly to see. And sure, sometimes it is overwhelming. But here's the thing: So is the beauty. Most of the time the ugly does not subside for us to see the beauty. Most of the time we just get tired of looking at it. We reach a level of pain we cannot or will not tolerate and make a decision to give our attention to something else. In that, we see the synchrony that has always been there. The peace, the beauty. Peace is quiet. Until we give it a voice.

LEENA MAGDI

* * *

Some truths are too painful to speak. But they can be heard. They can be read. That's what writing does for me.

* * *

It's interesting how grief works. We can be in the midst of a violent governmental overthrow, death teasing every day. We hear about people dying all the time. We see it. And it stirs something within us. The part of us that is shared. What is humane in each person. But grief does not make a full appearance until death touches a part of us. Brushes past us. Gets so close that our entire lives are changed. That is what happened to me the night of August 11, 2022. The night my brother was murdered.

MOURNING AIR

I remember being there
the shore
I remember seeing the sunset
Thinking how beautiful endings can be
Even more so because of how much they resemble
beginnings
I remember feeling the water
The feeling of water

It's different now
In the waves
In the middle of it
I don't feel the water anymore
I don't get wet anymore
I am constantly drowning
Constantly treading
The sun just seems like a glaring light
I can't tell if it's setting or rising
I don't see the beauty
I can't feel the water
I can only feel the crushing weight of the waves
This is my grief
And I don't know if I'll ever make it back to shore

LEENA MAGDI

* * *

Growing up in California, with its open minds and open valleys, infused in me a feeling of ease in being, a breeze of freedom that made it hard to adapt anywhere else.

home is not where you learn between rock and hard place
life will teach you that lesson
home is the conviction bred in you that assures you
recognize the lesson and only have to learn it once
home is the solid, fertile, soft ground you plant your feet in
home is your grounding
it is your benchmark
it is the place you come to when life tries to ruin you
it is your safe place
and it has to be **in** you
force can't teach that
only Compassion can

MOURNING AIR

My dad had a habit of obsessively replaying songs he loved in the car until someone urged him to stop. He and my mom would sing out loud to songs up to eight minutes long, over and over and over, up and down the Bay Area coast. Michael Jackson's greatest hits, Al Kabli, and Umm Kulthum were some favorites. It's been years since I've left the Bay, over a decade since my parents moved back to Sudan, but when I think back to my childhood, one of my clearest memories is their music: Umm Kulthum, my mom's love for 96.5 KOIT on the I-880 during our morning drives to school. Michael Jackson on the 680 when going to visit our uncle in Tracy on the weekends. Majida El Roumi's voice echoing over the Bay Bridge, singing Nizar Qabbani, words unlike any other.

For me, the Bay was a place unlike any other.

In my dreams, I often find myself back in our house in Milpitas. It is one of my mind's constant homes. Since then, I've discovered many homes to belong to. But that one holds dear, still.

And though I wasn't born in California, that is where I came to be. I was about five years old when my parents moved to the U.S. The first five years of my life belonged to Sudan. As an adult, I gave Sudan about the same amount of time: five years as a child, four years as an adult.

LEENA MAGDI

Sudan never asked much of me. But she took a lot.

How lucky are we to not be tied to one story
One place
One life
That we do not have just one home
that we have traces of different languages and cultures
that we are different stories
in different contexts and tongues
with equal belonging
how lucky are we to be able to choose
and create something new:
Nile-infused Pacifics

MOURNING AIR

* * *

Truth is, I never truly felt home in Sudan. Not until my brother was killed. Strange, isn't it? You would think the opposite would be true. That would surely make more sense. But I never felt like I belonged. My brother did. And it didn't come naturally to him either. But he wanted to belong. So he did. He created a community. He learned the language, the customs. He only internalized the best, and he tried to alchemize the damaged. My brother was an active force. He never stopped believing in Sudan. He never stopped believing in the people. He believed in the good, fiercely, when all we could see was bad. He understood, early on, that good and bad exist in synchrony.

After he was killed, belonging to Sudan, to the land that held my brother, was the only thing that felt like home. But just eight months later, the same forces that killed him forced my family and thousands of other families to leave everything behind and flee the country. Only country wasn't just country anymore. To many, it was the only home they had ever known. To all, it was generational homes. It was porches that held babies' steps, homes that fathers built, bricks with grandfathers' prints. Golden braids that told stories of dances passed down from mother to daughter, sister to cousin, daughter to mother to daughter. The golden braids from my mother given to her by her mother. These were the blueprints. Culture rich enough to carry different languages. Culture bold enough to transgress seas. A generous culture, a stubborn culture, a binding culture. Like the Nile, the Blue and White.

This is my Sudan. The soil that held my brother. It is the land that witnessed his last steps. The air that carried his last breath.

Where could I go from here?

What will be left of us
When home becomes four walls
When a roof over your head doesn't guarantee their
bullets won't get you lying in your bed
When country is family and family is country
And family bears witness while country is in mutiny
Because they've been eating away at the land
While the people are starving
And now they're eating away at the people
Throwing them in our beloved blue
In our beloved white
Making it a sea of red
Making it a sea of dead
Where bodies float despite the weight tied to their feet
When mass murder becomes the answer to a call for peace

MOURNING AIR

Truth turns to salt on the bricks tied to feet
So the Nile refuses to swallow what they force her to eat
Because the deeds of devilish men weren't made for her to keep
When the lives of innocent men are bought and sold for cheap
And homes turn to walls that crumble in defeat

> *What will be left of us*
> *When morning comes*
> *And the sun comes to collect*
> *All that can't be undone*

—Leena+Hamoodi

* * *

Betrayal comes in many flavors, and each one leaves us with a different aftertaste. Something we must work to cleanse our palate of. Wherever safety exists exists the risk of betrayal. We cannot have one without the other. They coexist in synchrony.

I believe there exist two general types of betrayal. Though they are both hurtful, in my opinion, one is far graver and harder to overcome.

The first, which may be the most common is, what I call a betrayal of expectations. We're in a relationship, business partnership, friendship, or any connection, with partners on different personal journeys, with different communication styles, different levels of growth and, most importantly, self-awareness. Eventually, due to these differences, or perhaps perpetuated by them, one party does something in pursuit of their personal journey that ends up betraying the expectations set forth by the relationship or partnership. It is not ill-intentioned, but it is self-centered. They did not mean harm, but they did not consider the other person. This type of betrayal is a symptom of a deeper issue, an indication, perhaps an invitation, to do the work, together or individually. It is not, however, the issue itself.

The other type of betrayal is a betrayal of trust. It involves one party entrusting the other with something—something physical, information, vulnerability, anything of that sort. The person who is entrusted takes that thing and weaponizes it against the other. This type of betrayal requires malicious intent. It is meant to hurt, to humiliate, to demean, and in extreme cases, to end.

Only one has the potential to destroy entire homes, entire countries.

* * *

MOURNING AIR

Ya binti, not all mistakes are equal. Everyone makes mistakes, it's fine. But some mistakes are fatal. Do not ever make a fatal mistake.

Something my father got from his father.

Romantic partners sometimes betray one another, friends can turn on each other, betrayal sometimes comes from kin, and sometimes a leader can betray an entire nation.

* * *

Nine on Saturday morning, the first explosion was close enough to jolt us out of sleep but not close enough to shake the house. The first one went off and I couldn't identify what the blast was. Gunshots came right after. This time I recognized the sound immediately. We had grown uncomfortably familiar with the sound of gunshots. Shootings at every protest, streams of gunfire, the bullets that killed my brother that had now become part of my sleep. The sound of gunfire had become part of our makeup as Sudanese citizens. Another bomb went off minutes later; this time it seemed closer. These blasts… This wasn't a typical protest. I ran down the stairs to my dad in the living room. Another one went off. This time, the house shook.

I remember putting my head down on the ground for *sujood* (prostration) and hearing a bomb go off. I remember the terror, feeling it coursing through my body like poison. Terror. One bomb. And then another. The walls shaking. Wondering if the next one would come through the bedroom wall, or the roof, or the living room. A missile had already hit the garage. The bullets were constant now, and a few had already pierced through my sister's room, our guest room. Another bomb. Not knowing where the next one would land, whether our house was next. That terror, it hovered amongst us like fog, forming a transparent hold over our minds, our homes, our every move. We couldn't quite see where it was coming from, but death seemed unescapable.

The phone rings
I hold my breath and brace for the worst
It's my sister
She is just checking on us, they're okay, she says,
Alhamdulillah
...Grace
The sound of gunshots hasn't stopped, but we have electricity and water
Grace
The house shakes again
Brace
The boys continue playing in the room
Small mercies, I think, small mercies...

Grace
A missile comes through the garage
Brace
Two people are in the garage
Brace
They are okay
Grace
I wake up two hours later in a frenzy to the sound of silence
Terrified at the silence
My shoulders etched in
Brace
The bombs start back up again
The planes... I hear the planes
Is this grace?
I cannot tell the difference anymore

* * *

I remember worrying where to sleep. We moved the mattresses to the floor, but I never knew which side of the mattress to place my kids on. The blasts... They enveloped us like a cloud from every direction.

Getting on the bus to leave Khartoum, I remember keeping the kids away from the windows in case a bullet or brick came through. It took us about eighteen hours to arrive at

Arqeen, one of the border crossings to Egypt. Arqeen is just that: a border crossing. It is not a city, town, or village. The closest area with livable conditions is four hours away. Arqeen is in the middle of the desert. There is no food in Arqeen, no water, no bathrooms. Upon arrival we were told there were fifty buses ahead of us, thirty inside the gates, and border patrol was processing two buses a day. We remained in Arqeen for four days.

There are makeshift shops in Arqeen that sell snacks: chips, Oreos, etc.
I take my kids to go buy some for themselves and my nephews.
They even have soda. No water, but soda.
Small mercies, I think, small mercies…
Grace.
Walking back, I notice my dad isn't sitting under the truck he typically uses for shade.
He's inside the bus.
The back of the bus. Where my grandmother sits.
Brace.
I notice a lot of people huddled around her.
Brace.
I run inside the bus and stand on the seat in front of my grandmother.
Brace.
Her eyes are closed.
Brace.

MOURNING AIR

My dad's hands on her shoulders,
on her face,
pleading for her to respond.
Her mouth is moving up and down, but she is not speaking.
Brace.
My sisters are crying.
Brace.
Someone get these kids.
I turn around and one of the boys is watching my grandmother.
I yell for one of my cousins to take him.
There's so much family around. Small mercies.
Grace.
I turn back to my grandmother; her mouth has stopped moving.
Brace.
My cousin leaves the bus and sits by the truck my dad usually spends the day under.
One of the ladies on the bus says she's a doctor and starts performing chest-compression CPR.
I think to myself, "*Her chest is moving up and down—her heart must be beating.*"
And then I hear someone say, "*It's her pacemaker.*"

I feel her neck for a pulse,
Brace…
I feel her wrist,
Brace…

LEENA MAGDI

Her hands are cold.

* * *

Death is promised. It is a certainty we will all one day face. Except for those who die young, all of us will feel the loss of a loved one in this world. Death touches us all in various ways across our lifetime, and in the end, we are all going. *"Finite as we are, each of us. We are further and closer all at once. Further from the goodbye and closer to the hello again. Time widens as it shrinks in space. Thank God."* —Jerrie

The last note on Hamoodi's phone read:

> *Memories carried,*
> *Over a bent shoulder*
> *Across valleys*
> *Through hills*
>
> *Age of mountains winds of heaven*
> —Hamoodi, August 9, 2022

I've been around the kind of death that speaks of origin. Like life has an origin. It doesn't just appear. Signs, dreams, and intuitive feelings that people receive before sudden and tragic accidents are too common to call coincidences. Perhaps those with terminal diseases could be justified for thinking about death. Or elderly people who may be nearing the end of life. But people who have died sudden, tragic deaths in their midlife or youth, who have no understandable reason to think about death, more often than not do. Where do those thoughts originate? *When* do those thoughts originate? I believe there is a place other than where we are. And that this is where we are for now. But it is not our home. And since we are all going, we must be going home. As long as we are living, we are also dying. Life and death exist in synchrony.

I have seen death. He has visited my home. We are close acquaintances. I do not fear death because I know he is near to me. We are not strangers. He is near to all of us. He knows my grandfathers. He knows my uncle. He knows my grandmother. He held my brother's hand as the angels took his soul. Death was there with us on the bus in Arqeen. Death was sitting next to my grandmother the whole time. He made my grandmother's exit peaceful. We never even saw him. Death waited until she said her final prayer before introducing himself.

* * *

We did not escape death; we escaped the war. My grandmother died on that bus in Arqeen. But had we stayed in Khartoum, she would have died on that Thursday morning just the same, perhaps due to different circumstances. Maybe it would have been a bullet. Maybe it would have been the roof collapsing. One way or another, death would have come that morning because it is a promised certainty. That is my belief. But because we survived, we must thrive. We must choose to extract value from the life we still have and not be upset about living. My time is surely coming. As sure as I am of the words I am typing, I am sure my time is coming. Just like your time and every single person's time is coming. And when our day comes, those we leave behind must celebrate our life and the lives they still have. Our familiar stranger waits for no one, and when our time comes, what will we have given to leave behind?

After seeing mountains crumble, we ask ourselves, how can we still stand? But really the question we must ask is, how can we stand still?

* * *

Home is not a place; neither is history, I said. *It's memories, stories told, and narratives passed down through generations. That is something that cannot be stolen. It exists within all of us wherever we are.*

Then, if not this, what makes you the saddest? she asked.

MOURNING AIR

Hamoodi... I whispered.

The hardest sentiment. The heaviest breath. A living statement.
My brother was a mountain. And he became one by helping others rise.

* * *

Eight months prior to the war, a different type of terror loomed. My brother was killed. My beautiful, kind, generous baby brother was shot by those sworn to protect the people. Betrayed by the men claiming to stand for security and freedom. Betrayed by the country he proudly and bravely stood for. My twenty-one-year-old brother was murdered, sitting in a car, by an armed national security officer dressed in plain clothing.

The ride to the hospital was silent. My cousin parked the car at the corner across the street from the emergency room. Walking up, I saw my dad standing outside. Someone was coming up to greet him; he lifted his hands, cupped in prayer to recite Al-Fatiha—the custom way to pray for the dead. My knees. I was still standing, but my knees were lead. I walked up to my dad; he held me in his arms and took me inside. My brother was lying on an emergency-room bed. Green sheets. He looked asleep. My mind trailed off; I was thirteen. My sister and I were sneaking away for school in the morning. Hamoodi was a baby then, three years old; he loved playing with us in the morning. My mind replayed the image of him running inside to get his ball from the garage as we slowly made our way out the front door. His laughing face bouncing back, blue-striped bouncy ball in both hands. My memory locked onto his face as he watched our car drive away through the window. I'm back in the emergency room. My knees are lead. My beautiful baby brother lies dead in front of me. Shot in the torso. My knees. My knees are lead.

Love,
I've cradled you
Held you close
I've carried you
In my heart
In my arms
I've watched you grow
I wasn't always as gentle as I should have been
But you, love, are binding
I don't know a life without you, love
I've only ever held you

MOURNING AIR

>My dear brother,
>My sweet brother,
>I don't know how to miss you
>I've never had to
>Not like this
>I've only ever carried you
>I've only ever cradled you
>And watched you grow
>I never thought I'd watch you go
>I don't know how

* * *

Mama, is Hamoodi one hundred years old? asks my four-year-old son, a question we go over with his older brother a few times a week.

No, I say, *he's not one hundred years old.*

Then how could he die?

I pause. *Sometimes young people die, Habeebi.*

On their own? asks his older brother, six years old.

I don't know how to respond. I don't know what is more terrifying for a six-year-old: that anyone can die suddenly, or that people can kill other people.

LEENA MAGDI

* * *

Untimely death. That is what it is called when someone dies an unexpected death. A tragic death. Someone who dies prematurely, for example. In youth. Suddenly. I think we call it *untimely* because it is unlike time. Or rather, unlike our *expectation* of time. We expect time to follow a natural order parallel to the order we see in nature. Seeds are planted, watered, nurtured; they grow, flowers bloom, they wither and then die. There is a natural procession of things. Life seems to have an order. Time seems to have an order. Time seems to *follow* an order. When it does not, we can no longer make sense of things. There is no order left to make sense of.

Losing a loved one is an experience that affects everyone differently. It is a perpetual pain that shakes the foundation of existence. Grief is a burning love. Loss and grief can alter many of our beliefs, and in some cases, new beliefs may begin. In my case, it began a new relationship with time. A misunderstanding. A betrayal.

MOURNING AIR

the days pass and I think to myself, God must be carrying
me because I've been standing still
I haven't left that hospital bed
my hands are still on your chest
still running through your hair
trying to pick things out of it
sometimes I hear myself speak, laugh, and I don't
recognize my own voice
I don't know who this person is
I'm still standing beside you
still whispering in your ear
still praying
I'm with you physically
I haven't left
I've been standing.
still.
sometimes I catch myself walking and my body gets
heavy
I have to stop
I slow down
it's like my mind suddenly realizes the movement and
can't process it
I can't make sense of things anymore
I can only stand still

* * *

Every loss is different. Every pain is different, colored by the love nurtured within the relationship. My mother's pain is her own, seen and felt only through her lens. None of us can feel or fathom what her loss is like. It is a special bond, one only she knows. My father's loss is his own, an altered relationship of father and only son. Each one of my sisters had a unique bond with our brother. Their loss is their own; I cannot begin to comprehend its depth. Each one of his friendships had a special dynamic, and each person's grief is at its peak. I think we belittle our loss and cheapen our love when we try to measure it as greater than or less than any other loss or pain. Every grief is experienced differently, and there are no shallow waters in grief. When grief comes, it does not come in slow. We do not halfway grieve. We cannot halfway grief. It is always the deepest end. Whenever and however grief comes, it comes at its highest peak. I cannot say one pain is greater than another, only that each pain is felt differently and deeply. For me, the loss of my younger brother is a tragedy that uprooted systems of imbedded beliefs about how the world operates. All of a sudden, I no longer felt safe. An urgency ensued. I no longer had time. I realized that perhaps I never did. Perhaps time did not betray me. Perhaps in trusting time, I betrayed myself.

MOURNING AIR

A few days ago marked four months since you left us
I'd be lying if I said that day felt any different than all the other days without you
It's been four months and one of the things I've come to learn is how trivial numbers are in time
It's been four months but it never stopped being the eleventh
Every day is that Thursday
Every hour is the eleventh hour of that night
And the end of the week doesn't signify the start of the weekend anymore
But the end of life the way we loved it
And the start of a life we don't know or understand
The start of a life where days pass but time stands still
A redefinition

* * *

The thing about tragedy is that we cannot get used to it no matter the number of times we encounter it. The war began about eight months after that night. Eight months after I stood, eyes fixed, fingers clenching my wrists, as the doctors searched for bullets in my brother's body. Eight months later bullets scattered on every street, every neighborhood, every home. A close friend of mine explained her experience with grief as one that "*breaks open.*" We cannot claim tragedy as ours alone. Tragedy belongs to everyone. It is a human experience. Like life, like death, like breath. In realizing this, our capacity for empathy expands exponentially. This is what I call the breaking-open. That is how I choose to see it. Tragedy breaks us, yes, but through the break, we open up to something much greater.

In Khartoum, we witnessed gruesome atrocities. The worst of humanity. We went to Arqeen and there was devastation. The kind that happens when people get desperate, when people get hungry. We saw death and other dreadful truths of life. Simultaneously, there were small mercies everywhere. What I was beginning to realize was that in every small mercy there existed infinite mercies. Within every infinite mercy was wisdom, deep human wisdom that only comes from being cracked open. Grief brings a knowing. Though it may be exhausting and devastating, it is a knowing I am grateful for. A revolutionary, transcendent capacity to see and connect with people beyond what is explicitly shown or heard.

* * *

The road to each border crossing, Arqeen and Halfa, is composed of miles and miles of barren desert. Still, every few hours there were people on the side of the road offering water, dates, and juice to those fleeing Khartoum. That humanity, that shared compassion, that was what kept us going. Unlike Arqeen, Halfa is a city; it has hotels and motels for people to stay in as they wait for their visas to cross into Egypt. Nonetheless, residents of Halfa opened up their homes to strangers by the dozens. They let them sleep there; they cooked for them. We stayed at someone's house in Halfa, not a relative or a friend, but someone who offered us a place to stay. That is the story of many. At the same time, there were border patrol agents and officers complicating matters because they felt like it.

Humanity and the lack of it can exist in the same moment, even in the same person. On our way out of Khartoum, we were stopped four times by RSF (Rapid Support Force) militias and one time by the military. My four-year-old nephew was sitting in the front seat of the bus. We purposely seated ourselves (women and children) in the front so that the soldiers known to stop and rob the men on the buses out of Khartoum would see a bus full of women and hopefully let us be. The same soldiers bombing houses, hospitals, and cars, killing people on the street, were the soldiers stopping the buses. Each time a soldier came inside the bus, my four-year-old nephew reached his hand out to shake the soldier's hand. Every soldier that stopped our bus shook my nephew's hand, joked with him, and turned around and treated every man on the bus with disrespect. Synchrony exists even in the horrific.

They say time heals
but all time really does is create space
and because space provides clarity
if the thing wasn't right, you then see it clearly
but when time is moving you further away from your loved one
and you are at a loss because of your loss
then time just becomes a space heavy
a space empty
an empty space
that isn't empty and isn't light
there is no healing here

* * *

Honesty is much more than simply speaking the truth; it is living in alignment with our truth. It is facing our demons, our fears, sitting with them, nurturing the shadow side of ourselves so that it may flow out. It is seeing that ugly and beauty go hand in hand. It is accepting the whole experience. It is continuing and committing to learning different parts of ourselves while giving others the grace to not have to understand. It is the courage to break open. That is the inhale, giving others the grace of their shadow side. Knowing when to walk away, with love. Knowing when to break a connection, without severing the tether of faith. It is transparency in action with oneself and grace in response to others. It is the courage to leave everything behind and start over; that is the exhale. Honesty is daring to continuously rediscover ourselves, shed parts of ourselves, and share parts with the world. It is trusting that in our vulnerability, we are stronger. In our authenticity, we give ourselves the opportunity to show up wholistically for ourselves and others. Honesty exposes the synchrony in life. It is alignment of purpose and action. And yes, honesty can sometimes be disruptive.

* * *

Sometimes when I'm having trouble sleeping
I go back to the last time I saw you
You were still already
You were cold already
You were there but you were no longer here
Still, I held you close
head on your chest
hands on your arm
waiting for a beat

Most days I have trouble sleeping
so I grab a pillow and place it under my chest
another one under my arm
I go back to the last time I held you
and wait for sleep

SECOND BREATH

Spirituality

My first two years back in Sudan came unexpectedly. It was December 2013, and I had just completed my undergraduate degree from San Jose State University and was on my way to start law school in the fall at Boston University. My parents had left California and gone back to Sudan with my younger siblings when I was in college. My dad suggested I defer law school and look for work in Sudan to spend time with the family. *It's been years since we've all been under one roof,* he said. I hated to admit it, and I tried hard to fight it, but part of me agreed with him. Deep down, I kept thinking to myself, *Three years of Hamoodi and Summer went by without me.*

I've always been really close to my siblings. When Summer was learning to spell, she insisted her name started with an *L*, like mine, not an *S*. For our mandatory community service in high school, Sara and I would volunteer at Hamoodi's elementary school and make sure his second grade projects made it to the center of every wall board decoration. I've never admitted this, but I never liked other people updating me about what was going on in Hamoodi's and Summer's lives. It made me feel like a stranger. So I stayed in Sudan for two years.

Two years of Sara and I working at different departments in the same company, getting to go to work and come back together.

Two years of coaching Summer for the talent show and watching Hamoodi's dance performances.

Two years of staying up late with my cousins, chitchatting in the bathroom downstairs so no one could eavesdrop.

Two years of late-night conversations with my parents, siblings, and cousins about souls and spirituality, the universe, light-years, God, energy, and connection, my dad insisting that everything could be explained through the theory of relativity.

Two years of writing Arabic phrases out in English on my phone to make sure I'd pronounce them correctly.

Two years of learning that to belong did not mean to fit in.

What I came to realize was that Sudan was always home for my parents in a way California never was. And because Hamoodi and Summer were so young when they moved back, it became that childhood home for them too. So when I came to stay with them in Sudan, it was like I was getting to know all of them through new eyes, in *their* home. There's a magic in places like Sudan, where culture is so prevalent and community is so significant. Where people are always around, willing and wanting to share in life with you, run errands with you, drink morning, afternoon, and evening tea with you, run to the emergency room with you. Where strangers will stop to help you change your tire. Where people give one another the benefit of the doubt.

It makes it hard to adapt anywhere else.

Sudan, for me, was, in Hamoodi's words, an *"acquired taste,"* but for my parents, and maybe for my younger siblings, it was where they truly felt home.

I stayed for two years, left for five, and came back. But those first two years left an imprint of home that said it is not time that bonds us to one another, or to the places we may find love. It is depth.

The second and last time I moved back to Sudan was in 2020, the summer after Covid. My time there ended about two and a half years later with the war. Moving back to that apartment in my grandfather's house, where my sisters and I once shared a room, this time with the addition of my two little boys, Hamoodi in the room next door, my parents across the hall, my aunt and cousin in the other room, it was cramped. But after Covid's isolation, it felt refreshing. It was restorative. And most of all, it was extra time, time none of us knew we needed.

LEENA MAGDI

* * *

there are some things I can't say out loud
so I write them down
I guess you can say there's an extension of myself found
in writing that isn't felt anywhere else
and there's one person who used to finish
my sentences for me
on paper
the ones I couldn't even share out loud
one person who is so bound to my truth that he
was able to voice it on paper
but his voice is no longer heard
and now I don't write the same
my heart is not the same
it's been so quiet
it's deafening
it's been so empty
it's heavy
I am not the same

* * *

I am the eldest of four. We are three girls and one boy. For those familiar with astrology, I'd tell you I have a third house stellium. In other words, my siblings play a significant role in many aspects of my life. And I love it that way. One of my sisters, Sara, is a year younger than me. Fifteen months, to be exact. She's always been my source of guidance, and everyone could see it. Fifteen years younger, my youngest sister, Summer, is joy encapsulated in a person. She pushes me and teaches me how to continue learning and growing in creativity, balance, and security.

My brother and I are ten years apart. In his life, he was my lighthouse. In many ways, he still is.

> I need you like moon needs sky
> like sun needs shine
> like voice needs heard
> like beauty needs eyes
> like happy needs self
> like soul needs God
> like heart needs touch
> like hands need purpose
> like back needs back

* * *

I have always had a complicated relationship with tradition and an even more complicated relationship with culture. And so, in a place where the culture is such an integral part of country and community, it resulted in a complicated relationship with Sudan and a difficulty in adapting.

But I never had a complicated relationship with my siblings. Things have always been clear as day when it comes to my siblings. If Hamoodi had a science fair project that he forgot about, Sara and I were up early, putting it together with him the day of. If Summer wanted me to stay home with her, I wasn't going out to the movies with my friends that night. If Sara wanted a dress I was planning on wearing, I'd pick out something else for myself. Looking back, I see just how pivotal a role they played in the small and big decisions of my life. They were *my own cocoon of sustenance.*

I remember we were driving down Airport Road to my grandmother's house (my mom's mom) in Emarat. And it hit me. It was a moment in the car. It was early 2014 and I had just made the decision to stay in Sudan. I knew that I may never go back to live in California. At least, not anytime soon. I accepted the fact that law school wasn't an option anymore; it was difficult enough to get in the first time, and I wasn't going to go for it again. I knew that version of me was gone. That the life that I envisioned for myself was no longer unfolding. So I wrote myself a letter, a goodbye letter. A love letter of sorts, to the person I thought I would become, the person I was, the version of myself that got me to this particular point in life.

MOURNING AIR

I danced today
I danced and I laughed and I cried
And I talked to a good friend and I talked to my parents
And I slept by my mother and I sat by my father
And I thought of you throughout the day, as I always do
You have gifted me freedom and authenticity
Two things change cannot take from me
I think letting you go will mold me
I'm sitting in this newfound vulnerability
and letting go of Cali
I don't know when I'll get to go back
But I'm embracing the idea that
I do not belong in just one place
I belong in every place
Wherever I go is home
Wherever God puts me is home
I am exactly where I am supposed to be
And I will continue to find happy here
I've got Sara
And I've got Hamoodi
And I've got Summer
And I'd be lost if I ever lost them
And I will always choose them over you
And I'm okay with that
And I have more family than I can count here
And that is more than just a blessing

LEENA MAGDI

> We had our time
> Thank God for that
> But I am finally content
> and thankful
> and home
> I'm home

2013 was the last year I spent in California.

I never did go to law school.

Seven years later, I went to Boston for the first time, with my dad, my sister Sara, and Hamoodi, for his first year in college.

* * *

When Hamoodi was killed, I felt like an essential part of me was taken. Was stolen. For that reason, it took me a long time to fully comprehend the loss of Sudan. I had already lost a home in Hamoodi. A home I carried in my soul. A pillar that made up all my other homes. Hamoodi was part of every home I ever built. He is part of me.

When we had to flee Sudan, my first thought was *But he's buried here.*

I contemplated digging his grave and taking his body. An absurd thought, I know. An impossibility, as so much time had passed.

But leaving Khartoum for me was leaving Hamoodi. It was leaving the chance to visit him at his grave every Friday morning. To water it. To bring him his favorite cologne. To talk to him about what we've been doing. To be able to say, *We're going to see Hamoodi tomorrow.*

My brother was my country. When all of Khartoum burned, he was all I could see.

It took me so long to wake up to the fact that the house my grandfather built, the room my sisters, sons, and I shared, the street Hamoodi and his friends used to carry mattresses across for his sleepovers in the room that barely fit his bed, the never-empty living room where a cousin or an uncle or aunt was always chatting about something or nothing, the big, loud birthdays, the front gardens, that house, that home was gone.

The home we ran to. They made us run from.

Sudan was where everyone came together.

LEENA MAGDI

And so, for a while, I foolishly thought I was coping better than others. But I was still only submerged in a specific piece of grief.

Sometimes
When you're engulfed in something
In the pit of it
It's hard to make poetry out of it
It's difficult to conjure up beautiful words
out of an ugly reality
That picture just can't be painted because
you cannot see it

And this for me has taken everything
It has taken my tools
I am canvas without brush
I am brush without paint
I am realizing
You have been my language
I know because now I am without words
You have been my math
I always knew then because I'd use your age
to remember mine
My geography, too, because you used to follow me around
and now I look for you everywhere
In everything I do
Geology

MOURNING AIR

Because our composition is the same
Made of shared minerals and particles that date back
before we ever shared a family name

Life gave me time before you
Time gave me life after you
But you are my words
My school and my home

* * *

There was a big part of me that wanted to die with Hamoodi. That wanted to curl up next to him. It was a feeling I couldn't help. Kind of like a sobering, harrowing acceptance or waiting for something. So much so that when the war came, I almost didn't mind staying in Khartoum. I didn't mind waiting for death. Only, I had my boys. They became my lifeline. After Hamoodi, most days I could barely engage in conversation. I didn't even want to. But I needed to get up, plan playdates and birthdays, make forts out of pillows, engage in life. I had faces that looked up at me, faces that looked up for me. Innocent eyes that looked to me and everything I did. I couldn't let them down. My boys gently kept me afloat. They kept me present. When my mind would wander somewhere in how things used to be, or how things would never be again, my sweet boys, unknowingly, drew me back to now. *Your eyes aren't smiling, Mama.*

My boys taught me to be explorative in how I do things. To pay attention to little things because that's where life happens. In the little moments. The simplest things. Missing the button on my shirt and hearing them giggle, standing an extra minute to wave bye as they slowly made their way, walking backwards, to their classrooms every school morning. Answering their questions about where Hamoodi was, if he could see us. They have taught me to face my grief so that we could navigate it together. They've shown me how souls connect. They have taught me how to hold space for love. They have taught me to slow down. I realized that they were learning how to view life through me. If my energy was communicating stress, that was what they would understand, that life was stressful, difficult, and rushed, even if my words were sweet. But if I was playful, exploring through the pain, maybe they'd learn to remain open, curious. Even when they were scared, they wouldn't give up.

My boys taught me to stay present, that our love is always present. That love, when true, is not bound to a particular expression or form, even in loss. It is not bound to certain memories or a certain time or place. Not by distance or circumstance. As long as we are sharing it, gifting it, it remains present.

MOURNING AIR

Even in your absence, you are so deeply felt.
I see you in T's fearlessness. His loud, heartfelt laugh.
B's curiosity. His nurturing nature and care for others.
S's tenderness. His eagerness to forgive.
A's humor. His desire to share in laughter with others.
You are so present in each and every one of your
nephews.

Death is interesting. Grief is a feeling of loss, of someone's absence. Yet it is ever present. Even in their absence, they are present. I think that speaks to energy. Speaks of energy. How it communicates. How we needn't be in the presence of one another to feel the presence of one another. We can be close and far, all at the same time. In synchrony.

* * *

on raising my boys. to. men

now
I'll make sure he feels safe
So that he recognizes safety
So that later he knows how to make others feel safe
So that when he's older he knows how to keep others safe
He will know the world's grandest delusion of forgoing
humanity for "masculinity"
and that that isn't masculinity at all
that real men hold steady like mountains
and stand tall like redwoods
real men hold space
hold hands
and hold hearts
he will know that to be worthy of respect he
must first be respectful
to be worthy of trust he must first be honorable
he is going to know that he is an active force
he is going to understand that that does not mean he has
to be forceful

The sun and the moon are the two luminaries in our solar system, our two sources of light, the sun being the primary source of light and metaphorically life, our essence, and the moon reflecting it, our source of light at night.

MOURNING AIR

My boys are my luminaries, not even in a metaphorical, cliché kind of way. But they give me light when I lack it and reflect my energy back to me, the ugly and the good, in a way that forces me to face myself. To dim but not burn. They are my source when I have none. If it weren't for them, I honestly think I could have willed myself to death, because after Hamoodi was killed, I had no interest in living. They have been my source of life.

* * *

Perhaps one of the most painful facts revolving around loss is that the world moves on afterwards. It must. What exacerbates sibling loss, and most losses, I imagine, is that people treat you like you are whole when an essential part of you has been taken. I am not the same Leena anymore because Hamoodi isn't here. It is like there is an inherent part of me that is missing, but only I see it, only I feel it. The rest of the world operates as if I am complete. I am the same, only I am not. I cannot be. Love between siblings is difficult to explain; I would not call it a thing *between*. We are a part of one another's history, key ingredients in one another's final piece. When one part is snatched away, the whole no longer resonates. It almost becomes irrelevant for a while. It cannot operate. It must find a new way to navigate. It's like taking a part out of the whole after it is complete. It feels unnatural. A retrograde. A hole within the whole.

LEENA MAGDI

I went to a yoga class yesterday
And honestly it was one of the best I'd ever been to
Maybe even the best
But I know I won't be going back
The instructor mixes yoga with a little bit of Pilates
I kept hearing your voice in every move
In every breath
How you used to laugh at me when I would work out and then come and join me
Then yell at me to stop
My body remembered when we did this together
When we would laugh about synchronizing breath to movement to muscle
I can't focus on my breath knowing you're not breathing the same air
I can't move the same way
I've lost that muscle

The thing about sibling loss is that it can easily go unnoticed. When I meet someone new now, they'll just assume I don't have a brother. I constantly find myself looking for ways to bring him up just so people know he was here. So he is not forgotten. To validate his existence and possibly make meaning out of his loss.

MOURNING AIR

A few days ago, I was registering my younger sister for school, and there was a section asking her to list her siblings' names and addresses. It took me about a minute to fill it out. I did not know what to write, whether I should include his name. I felt I would be betraying him if I did not. But what would I write?

Bringing him up changes the tone of any conversation, and I do not do it with that intention. I do it to keep him alive, to keep his memory alive. But I know not everyone is programmed that way. I know for some their own discomfort with grief keeps them from engaging with it when it shows up. Especially this kind. No one wants to see it. No one wants to trigger it. No one wants to be there when it resurfaces. I know some people tie him to his tragedy. And that is what I want to change. He is not what happened to him. I love talking about him even if it does elicit tears; I know they will eventually lead to laughter. Because the two do exist together. The gravity of this grief validates his greatness, his love.

* * *

My dad used to say that what worried him the most about Hamoodi was that once he believed in something, he no longer made room for fear. Hamoodi had a certain kind of courage that, for a father, was terrifying to see in a son so young, in a place so volatile. The days when people were out protesting, and the police were using tear gas, shooting protestors, Hamoodi was out protesting. It always caused arguments with my dad. My mom was terrified but also proud. She went with him once. They shared the same conviction and courage.

* * *

As close as I was to my brother, that is how close I feel to death. Not close as in my time is near, but rather close as in death is a close friend because a part of my heart is with him. I think about death every day. Not in a frantic, *oh my God, I'm going to die* kind of way, but in a *let me make this day right* kind of way. I no longer fear death. This closeness I feel has enriched my taste for life. Savoring each moment has become paramount. I understand now that insignificant moments do not exist. The little things *are* the big things. The soft way Hamoodi would squeeze my shoulders every time he'd hug me. The Spanish latte I brought him on that last day. How I messed up the order and brought him an iced latte instead of a hot one. How he told me he wanted it iced anyway. I knew he didn't. He knew he didn't. But he told me he did so that I wouldn't feel bad.

MOURNING AIR

<pre>
                    I wonder
             When it's our time to go
         Will we mourn those we've left behind
    Will we miss them the way we now miss those who have
                     left us
      Or will we rejoice in knowing they'll soon join us?
         If so, then why not start celebrating now?
            Why not celebrate the life they've lived
               And the lives we've yet to live
                   Forevermore
                    Together
</pre>

Love is in the little things. The pieces. It is thoughtfulness. It is foundational. It anchors. It is the anchor. The subtleties. Looking at someone while speaking to them. Showing up in the quiet chaos. Following the whispers. It is unseen support. It is being there, unwavering, in the times that are unrecognized. It is the people left standing with us in the eye of the storm. It is remembering when others forget. When others would understand that we forgot. Love is value. The special handshakes between me and my sons. Reminding them when they forget. Reminding me when I forget. Love is celebrating together. Little things. Giving extra tips whenever I can. Pausing to feel the breath in my body.

LEENA MAGDI

If today is my last day, I want it to be a good one. That's how I've been living each day since my brother passed. Fully here but knowing that at any moment, I could be gone. Or anyone else around me, for that matter. The extra five minutes on the phone with my cousin, waiting for my sisters, cousins, mom, and dad to come home so we can sit together and watch the same TV show. When one of my kids is throwing a tantrum and I lose my temper, I remember and make a point to apologize, to connect, to make it right. These are the moments that matter. These are the moments that color our big picture.

I want my kids to remember in color
I don't want black and white for them
I don't want their childhood to be a bunch of grays
I want them to remember the taste of laughter
Unkempt and infinite
I want them to know all the backs that bent to make sure
they knew how to stand tall
And that those same backs would break to break their fall
I want them to know all the women that made them
And held them
And raised them
I want them to know their names
I want them to know that God is always
Always here, always good

MOURNING AIR

I want them to know that family is always open doors
open minds
open arms
and open hearts
I want them to know that *"roots precede fruit"*
So they know that we are with them in everything they do

* * *

Love lives on long after we are gone. The love we leave behind is what keeps us alive in this world. The love we leave behind is what keeps our loved ones going long after we are gone. When we love someone, and the love is true, it grows with every day. Some of us know to learn how to express that love, be it through words, a shared laugh, a knowing look, locked eyes, quality time. Whatever the modality, we pour our love into one another. Losing a loved one does not change that reality.

In a strangely similar way, when our loved ones are no longer with us, our love for them continues to grow despite the lack of new and present interactions with them. True to the nature of synchrony in life, the longer the grief, the deeper the love; they seem to move in parallel timelines. The greater the distance in memory, it seems, the greater the love. Sometimes it can feel like they're right here with us; we can imagine their reactions to certain scenarios, hear their laugh. Other times, however, the emptiness is bitter enough to taste. Every experience in their absence brings forwards a new wave of love that has no place to go until we create a space for it.

Did you see the video of Jon Snow on *Jimmy Fallon*?
I could hear your laugh
Almost instinctively, I went to share it with you
It made me laugh and just as quickly cry

I've been having so many conversations with you
since you left

Did you hear the J. Cole feature?

I feel you in those lyrics. Hope.

But today
it hit me that you were already gone when
this song came out
You never heard it
You won't hear any others
We won't talk about them anymore
I've been whispering myself to sleep
Telling myself I'm talking to you
I've been praying you'd visit me in my sleep
I've been longing to hear you talk back

MOURNING AIR

> Did you get the video?
> Did you hear the song?
> Because I heard you laughing

* * *

Love deserves to be shared. Grief this great speaks of mountains. And if nothing else, mountains lift. So, if we're carrying it, it must mean it has the power to lift others. Grief this great cannot be kept quiet. Love this great must be given. To honor our loved ones, we can try to put our love for them into something. Our grief towards something. In service of something.

> on the days I have news to share
> or something good to say
> the pain digs even deeper
> I know it's here to stay
> your absence is a presence all on its own
> a faithful companion
> that makes sure our thoughts, and maybe our hearts
> are never left alone

The creative process is both transformative and transcendent. If we give ourselves permission, the expressive process can be as well. Grief returns us to the elements, to our base. Grief invites us to get know love through all its forms. In all its forms.

LEENA MAGDI

Through the elements. To explore our own experiences of love with our loved one and rediscover how to love them and share them in new ways.

These days I'll go back to live photos
From the days you were still here
I'll go through all the pictures
Even ones you're not in
And I'll replay them and listen closely
Straining and praying to catch a little bit of you in the background
Someone told me I'm not letting myself grieve
What they don't understand is
I'm not concerned with grieving
I am trying to continue loving you in your new form
In your new home
In your new state
And this is the only way I know how
So sometimes that looks like listening for your voice in pictures you're not a part of
Sometimes it looks like having one-sided conversations with you
Where I vent and vent and vent
And you just listen
Sometimes it looks like trying to get myself to not think about you because I will overflow once I do

MOURNING AIR

Love does not end when life ends
It continues to expand, yearning for a home to belong to

There is a theory about elements and alchemy in astrology. In a nutshell, it says that we need a combination of compatible elements for any kind of transformation to occur. Some elements move energy and emotions while others gently transform them. Water and air move but do not change on their own. Earth and fire transmute but do not move. For transformation, we need to get to know all the elements. Fire and air, earth and water.

In grief, our loved ones become earth. But we are no longer grounded. We are made of water. And if we do not give ourselves permission to pour into something, our grief will drown us into ourselves. Grief is a fire. It burns. Why do people say "hold space"? Because space holds air, and air holds energy. We need air to breathe. We need energy to communicate. Healthy expression keeps the air around our fire stable. With the right nurturing, fire doesn't have to burn; it can warm. It can illuminate.

That is what the expressive process does for grief. It pours into the Earth. It makes something new out of the love and the loss. It tames the fire. The eruptions still occur, but they are effusive. Expression can look different to different people: Some love to paint, some love to tell stories, some write, some finish works their loved one never had the chance to finish, some make the intention every day to remember them in what they do. Expressing our grief into something gives us a tangible thing to center us back to gravity. To Earth. To our loved ones.

>
> they say we're made of water
> that we are mainly water
> but I have no water in me
> I am all fire and earth
> some air
> maybe that is why it is hard for me to swim in waters this deep
> why I am constantly treading
> I wasn't made to swim
> some say I was made to burn
>
> No.
> I say I was made to warm
> I say I was made to fly

* * *

Culture has made it taboo for us to talk about our grief and to share in it. I think when we have something bigger than ourselves to hold on to, we're more likely to see the humanity of our calamity. That it is indeed a human thing that is shared. Maybe not in the details but certainly in the experience.

Grief is not a short-term experience. It is enduring. And so, we must recognize that we, too, are enduring. I view grief as a reminder of the love I have to be shared. To actualize it, not just feel it. To tell the people around me every chance I get how much I love them. To thank people. To actually, truly laugh out loud. To make eye contact. I love my brother more than I can ever say. Therefore, I try to make something palpable out of that love, with hopes that the love he elicits is felt by many. In that, I believe, there is longevity. In that, there is endurance. There is synchrony.

* * *

My mom is one of the most spiritual people I know. She always says prayer is our connection, our link, or *sila*, to our Creator, to the Divine. A conversation with God. That when we stand in prayer, or speak in prayer, to imagine we are speaking to God in any form and language. To approach people by looking for the piece that is from God in them, their *rooh*, and speak to that. To turn everything we do into a form of prayer and watch how the universe starts to reciprocate its magic. She prays with every breath. Whenever any random person, family or otherwise, needed anything, I'd see my mom rummaging through closets in the house. She'd give anything away, knowing the universe gave back tenfold. And it usually does. Through my mother, I learned what it meant to connect with myself so that I can connect with God. To get really quiet and drown out the background noise and see the part of any situation that is Him. I learned how to be fluid. How to flow. When calamity hits, it's these little things that come back and ground us: looking for God, knowing He's there, even when it doesn't seem like it. Even when it's ugly and things and souls…have been taken. We know He's there because we've practiced finding Him. Everything is a prayer.

We can live life like everything's a coincidence or live it like everything's designed for us. Live it like magic is everywhere, and it will be.

* * *

Such wonder is the Nile: a goddess as old as Africa itself, whose waters run as deep as the unknown and as fluid as time. Her conjunction of White and Blue ironically makes up the Red in my body, for I am forever drawn to her nomadic essence and lunar pull. Seeing her curves carve the earth thin at one place and wide at another, I would think that such is life: With one hand it takes, and with the other it gives. A

MOURNING AIR

truth so genuine that God has imprinted it in the very land that encompasses our origin. One that I have come to readily accept.

Much can be learned through the intricacies of Mother Nature. Just as a shimmering waterfront hides the murky depths beneath it, so, too, is the human psyche. The Nile's beauty is not tainted by the creatures that lurk within it but rather completed by their presence. That is the essence of our own demons. They are not pollutants of our minds but rather their natural inhabitants. Even as the beasts of the Nile constantly break the concealment of her beauty, so must you embrace the periodical surfacing of strife. Trust the certainty underneath Nature's tender course of chaos.
Grow to acknowledge the seasons of your heart.
Be fluid, like a river.

—Hamoodi, August 12, 2020

THIRD BREATH

Love of Learning

It's 2007. We're in Milpitas, my mind's favorite home. I slide the back passenger window down. *Hamoodi, we're going to Walgreens. We'll be right back. Baba's home.* Sara's in the front seat with Mama, and Summer's in her car seat in the back with me. Hamoodi's about six or seven years old, playing basketball in the street with the neighborhood kids. They're a little older than he is, nine or ten years old. He turns to look at me and misses the ball as they throw it to him. *Hamoodi, you really can't catch!* shouts one of the kids. Mama starts to drive off. *Maybe you just can't throw!* I yell back. I hear Hamoodi laughing as the car turns the corner.

* * *

> *Inaudible screams at the Soul's behest*
> *The Heart lets out and shrinks into regrets;*
> *Solemn requests to God a lighter test*
> *Fallen to a deaf ear,*
> *Heard nonetheless*
> *Despair not, for your being is to Live*
> *To Live and to Laugh and to Love, in full*
> *You are God's to judge, His alone to forgive*
> *Trust His mercy, His Love is merciful.*

LEENA MAGDI

And to truly Live you must Love freely
Allow your Heart to scream, it must be heard
By the heavens, if not your ears only.
Despair not, the Seven Skies have conferred
And concurred to relieve you of your gloom
Their only request: Plant flowers to bloom

Look to the Earth and accept her Seasons
The Winters of your grief will end in Spring
So tend to your gardens with known reason
That buds will wake and Summer they will bring.
Look to the stars and set your Heart ablaze
Let the angels know their call was heeded
Accept all love in every form and phase
And the World's wonders will be yours indeed.
Look to the Nile, such wonder is the Nile
Gentle and loving, her tender curves carve
Smiles into the earth and grace it fertile:
Notice around her life is to revolve.
Look to God and applaud his creation
Know, you deserve the same admiration.
—Hamoodi

MOURNING AIR

My brother wrote that poem just months before he was killed. I remember when he shared it with me. We used to always share our writing with each other. Any kind of writing—schoolwork, poems, random stuff. To read, hype each other up, edit—any kind of support. He actually edited my master's capstone thesis before I sent it to my adviser and again before I submitted the final version. I remember reading the above poem and thinking, *"Wow, Hamoodi is such an incredible writer."* I never stopped to think about what he might have been moving through. I did not consider what was plaguing his mind, his heart. I didn't ask him if anything was wrong. What compelled him to write like that? That is something that haunts me to this day. Did he feel something he couldn't explain? How could I, his older sister, the person he used to come confide in, not notice? How could I not see? I never even thought to ask.

* * *

I'm having migraine attacks
The kind that put me in the hospital
The kind I haven't had in years
I'm bleeding when I shouldn't be
My knees feel as if they're slicing open to keep me upright
My hands... They tremble sometimes
My heart cannot carry this load on its own
So my body is taking its turn

LEENA MAGDI

* * *

We are programmed to resist the idea of being broken. That resilience is the ability to bend but not break. I disagree with that notion. I believe that notion puts insurmountable pressure upon ourselves. Sometimes the worst happens. Unimaginable suffering happens all around us. And I've learned that yes, we do break. But the story does not end there. The question isn't whether we break. It is what we do with the break. We can break down or break open. I see resilience as the capacity to expand, not just to overcome but to grow. It is not bouncing back, as we cannot go back to what we were before. It is bouncing forwards. Harder. Stronger. Kinder and more beautiful.

I cannot deny the break that loss engenders. But broken does not have to mean destroyed. Broken does not have to mean defeated. Kintsugi is a form of Japanese art created by putting together broken pottery using gold to fill in the cracks. It is based on the philosophy that by embracing imperfections, rather than discarding something once it breaks, we can rebuild and recreate something beautiful and, more importantly, something stronger.

The same concept can be applied to our greatest challenges. The philosophy of kintsugi is very much parallel to the idea of post-traumatic growth. The cracks responsible for our greatest wounds can be filled with gold. We can transform from our adversities into stronger, kinder, more empathetic versions of ourselves. Does that explain, justify, validate, or belittle the adversity? Not in any way. All it does is give us power to move forwards, to add value to our lives and that of others.

Post-traumatic growth is defined as the concept that through adversities that shake us to the core and challenge our beliefs about the world, we can be pushed to grow. Adversities that break who we are, who we used to be. Through post-traumatic growth, we develop a vulnerable yet stronger narrative. The crack is the breaking-open that offers us an opportunity to grow.

It is not the trauma itself that leads to change but how we interpret the trauma—what we do with the crack—that causes the change. My brother was killed and none of us could have foreseen that. But him being taken so suddenly has guided me to make more concentrated efforts to pay attention to the people I love. To my sons, to my sisters, to my nephews, to my parents, to my friends. We can sink into our grief, our anger, and that would be understandable, or we can use it and increase our capacity for compassion towards the people we still have in our lives.

* * *

It's two years later. On the anniversary of your death. And in my mind's eye I see everything exactly the way it was that day. I feel everything exactly the way it was. In truth, I replay the little happenings of this day a lot more than I'd like to admit: you keeping me company, lying down on Summer's bed, while I sat on the floor, reorganizing the boys' closet; laughing about why they call pop-it toys *pop-its*. Going to the coffee shop in the afternoon. You napping in the afternoon. You leaving and coming back. Leaving again. Your beige *jalabiya*. Waiting for you to come home so we could put the laundry away together. I didn't even see you leave the second time. The last time.

Me standing by that emergency room bed. Green sheets. Shocked. Silent.

Only, in my mind, I'm not standing. I'm on my knees.

In my mind, I'm screaming.

Two years have passed, and when people ask how I'm feeling, *Alhamdulillah*, I say,
I'm okay.

But I'm screaming, Hamoodi. I'm on my knees.

* * *

MOURNING AIR

Understanding how grief manifests in our own lives allows us to reclaim our power in those parts of our life—to take back the reins of control. Our experiences and traumas can be the wind that shakes and rattles us, but they will not determine the direction of the boat.

I wore pink today
I wore pink today and I danced with the boys
and I sang in the car with Sara
like we all used to do
playing old songs we love
I saw one of my favorite poets
she talked about trying to find home
in time
I thought about how I always chose to come back to
where you were because you were there
you and my favorite summer. time
in every event that happens my mind trails back to a time
where you were still here
when you were still here
and I think to myself
I don't know how to reach you
I'm stretching, breaking, bending, trying to figure out how
to reach you

* * *

LEENA MAGDI

It was the summer after my first year in college, when my parents, Hamoodi, and youngest sister, Summer, moved back to Sudan. My sister Sara and I stayed in California. That summer, Sara and I went to visit the family in Sudan at the house in Garden City with my aunt and all our cousins. It was a full house. I remember one of our cousins was having a bad day. She's much older than Hamoodi, but they were really close. She was lying down with her hands covering her face and wouldn't talk to anyone. Hamoodi came into the room, sat next to her, tried to make a few jokes, poking fun at her in his usual lighthearted way. He would tease her, try to make her laugh, but she just wouldn't respond. So he left. There was this song she really liked; she would replay it in the car all summer. He came back in the room with the iPod we all shared, played her song, put the headphones next to her ear, and left the room. He was ten years old at the time.

How eerie it is to remember the times before someone's
existence
And to equally know the times after their death
To know life before they came
And after they left
To know
Intimately
The framework time assigned their stay
Their life

MOURNING AIR

But....
If truth transcends time
Then is it life we are measuring or just time?
Are we to bother with time at all?
Does it matter?
True life transcends it
It started before and it continues after

* * *

A few months after my brother was killed, I started teaching high school students. I didn't realize it then, but retrospectively I recognize a part of me went searching for people who reminded me of him. To be around young people, to be able to speak to them how I spoke to him. I told myself I wanted to do something that added value. But I ended up gaining the most value. The students I taught breathed life back into me.

One of my students asked me how my brother's death affected me. The complete answer is that it has changed me on a fundamental level. My brother is my roots, he is my country, he is my home. After Hamoodi, everything appeared in its transient form. The war solidified that truth. Living in a world without him has caused me to treat life with a little more urgency, to treat people with a little more grace, to treat myself with a little more love and accountability, to allow myself the capacity to add value.

To be softer in speech. To laugh harder with my boys. To yell a little less often. Let things slide. I have learned to be intentional, to pause, to breathe. To appreciate the breath, smile and look people in the eye when they speak to me.

Compassion is the capacity to feel what another is feeling coupled with the desire and willingness to help—that was the sentence that my eleventh grade English teacher kept on the board in her classroom every day of class in all of her classes every single year. She had it up my year, and she had it up the following year when my sister had her same English class. What she highlighted for us was the *desire and willingness to help* aspect. *Compassion is active,* she used to say. *It moves you to act no matter how small the act may seem.* My brother was compassionate. He was loved because he was loving. He was lovable because he was giving. He was brave. And he was so very compassionate.

Our capacity to share in humanity with one another is infinite. Outside of our physical limitations, our ability to withstand, to hold, to endure, to love, and to give is elastic. If any of us were told of our struggles before their time, we would have struggled to conceive how we'd carry them and then carry on. But we do. Our capacity to endure stretches and we survive. We have the ability to thrive. Our capacity was designed with elasticity so that we can thrive. When we feel we are being pushed to our limit, that we cannot take it, that it is crushing, it is because we are growing, we are expanding, we are breaking open.

Hold love of people in your hands and the love
will overflow
When we hold people in our hearts, we will never feel full
Because our hearts weren't made to house people
Our hearts were made for everlasting Light
We are not meant to hold people in our hearts
We're meant to hold them **to** our hearts

* * *

Trauma happens. That's a part of being, a part of living. But the decision to learn and grow from it is entirely on us. This is true for big traumas and little traumas. All of our experiences, the good in parallel with the difficult, carry lessons meant to push us further and higher on our journeys. In that, we find the synchrony.

Time moves on whether we move in growth or not. Life will move on. Good experiences will follow, and so will the difficult. But if we do not stop, reflect, learn, and grow, we will not engage with the good wholeheartedly. We will hold back, afraid, waiting for the other shoe to drop. Equally, we will not have the grace required to handle the inevitable challenges when they arise. We will break down, not open, every time.

* * *

LEENA MAGDI

the summer air here is humid
nostalgic almost
one can say it's filled with tears
almost like she remembers
like she holds in her the breathes of summers past
all the laughs echoed in the clouds
all the smiles carried
summers are not light here
but they are full
they are lasting
they are special

I feel him here
so...physically
almost as if he actually is
I hear his voice

I wonder sometimes if he ever left

some days that gives me peace
some days it breaks me more

* * *

If we pay attention to life synchronies, we'll realize that every moment prepares us for our biggest, most trying moments. Each of our moments is built to help us move through those unspeakable times. Though time may seem against us, fate is not. Synchrony always exists, and because it does, we are able to move forwards. Not overcome because grief is not something we can just get over, but we can move with time, and it is because we notice these little things. These little things the universe gifts us along the way. I watched an interview about death with my brother a few days before he was killed. It was a woman sharing her story about losing her partner who had been killed a few years prior. Months after, her words from that interview came back to me. Her loss was different; she lost a partner, a lover, a father to her youngest child. I lost my little brother. But her words resonated. They hit home. Love taken; life stolen. It is a different type of pill to swallow. My brother and I watched her together.

Life stolen is a unique pain for those still living. It is piercing on some days, dull most days, reminiscent of our shared humanity and our shared mortality every day. It is terror. It is a reminder that we cannot control, nor can we protect. It is nuanced fear. There can be acceptance here, but standing alongside it is rage; looming above it is fear. There is no reconciliation because it is not just us and our Creator; there is another human being responsible, another person who shows no sign of guilt, regret, even shame. There are power dynamics that abuse their power, systems in places of power that hold no remorse. Systems in places of blame that place blame on the innocent. Irresponsible systems reigning unaccounted for. Life stolen is confusion. It is wanting to have faith and struggling. It is pained love, confused love, betrayed love.

The thing about betrayal is that it comes from within the walls of safety; a close friend, a spouse, a safe environment, officers meant to protect the people, country, laws. It is not just us and our Creator. These are people and places alike that we expect to be protected by. Betrayal, therefore, becomes unexpected. The closer the person or the greater the perceived safety, the greater the risk, the harder the fall. Only, it does not feel like a fall, but more like an unexpected shove, a sudden drop, a fatal stab. In those circumstances, forgiving often seems like a betrayal of self.

Forgiveness is often confused with making space.

We make space for those who mean no harm.

However, we can still forgive those who did while never making space for them again.

We cannot allow those who have chosen to abuse their place of power a chance to claim that position once more. We cannot make space for them anymore.

I can accept what's happened, but it's my responsibility to try to fix what's broken for future generations. Even if that sometimes just looks like speaking up, or planting distance, refusing to participate in certain routine activities, kneeling. If a system is broken, the entire system needs to be replaced, not just the people representing it.

Forgiveness, for me, means I've forfeited my right to seek revenge on the specific person to our Creator, because we belong to Him and unto Him we shall return. It does not mean I will sit idly by while the same patterns continue to potentially harm others. Forgiveness requires us to attempt to enact some change. Firmer boundaries. Clearer values. Otherwise, we only become part of what hurt us. Part of the system that wronged us. Part of a system in which the value of a human life is not based on our shared humanity.

A corrupt system allowed a trained officer to believe he could purposely shoot and kill my brother, an innocent, unarmed civilian. A corrupt system allowed him to believe whatever he did was justified. And even if that officer had been convicted, it would not be enough, because it's the system that gave him that power and the right to abuse it. He is one of many.

Unfortunately, this abuse of power leads many families in many places all over the world into grieving a life stolen.

LEENA MAGDI

What happened to my brother has given me the courage to speak up and say it shouldn't ever happen to anyone. *Never again for anyone.*

Forgiveness and second chances do not have to go hand in hand.

Maybe there lies, in forgiving those who have most wronged us, a door.
A tip of the scales.
A gateway to something higher. To the best of company.
Maybe in forgiving, we are given much more.

Because when we zoom out, everything stripped down is just us and our Creator.

for. giving.
what are we giving up
and who are we giving it up for?

there's a grieving that comes with loosening the grips
on our anger
with letting go of the right to stay in that place

MOURNING AIR

what parts of ourselves are we so tightly holding on to
when we hold on to all that hurt?
who will we be when we release?
when you've been wronged or abused
when so much has been taken from you
you hold on to that anger and you think
by holding on to it, you're reclaiming that little bit of you
that you have left
but the ironic thing is
that anger was never yours
that anger was given to you

remember who you are
remember what you're made of
I'm not asking you to put it down, because Lord knows
you're big enough to carry it

I'm only asking
is it what you want to be carrying?

so I ask again
what are we giving ourselves when we hold on to that anger?
and who are we doing it for when we forgive?

Forgiveness is allowing ourselves the air to breathe.

To free the grips of anger and exhale.

It is release without surrender.

* * *

There's a section in the Quran, chapter ninety-four, verses six to seven, that state, *"Indeed with hardship is ease."* It is repeated twice, consecutively. *"Indeed with hardship is ease."* Not after, not before, not under specific circumstances or conditions—*with*. Our peace exists within all of our experiences, even our most painful moments. That in itself can be painful to acknowledge, that in our tragedy, there can be peace. But that is the beauty of being. There exists synchrony in every moment. Otherwise, we would not be able to keep moving, to keep living.

* * *

Sometimes I try to force this day out of my memory. But it constantly creeps back in. I wish I had a good reason for getting so angry. But even then, I don't think it would make it any less trivial. I think I wanted Hamoodi to drive me to Qahwa Republic, this coffee shop I really liked. It was late and I didn't like driving at night those days. There were random military stops. People were getting robbed in their cars. I didn't want to go alone. Hamoodi had his boxing class and didn't have time to take me, bring me back home, and go to the gym. I'm pretty sure that was the issue. Doesn't seem like much of an issue now. But I made it a big deal. A really big deal. I told him he was selfish and petty. I didn't tell him I was scared to go alone. I just said I didn't want to. He must have talked to Summer, because he came in the room, saying he didn't know I was scared and that of course he'd take me anywhere. *Come on, let's go.* But I was so upset, I wouldn't even turn around to look at him. *Lon aini lei. Lon look at me. Look at me, please...*

There are moments that play back in my mind's eye
every now and again
Like a scene from a movie
Moments
I couldn't tell you what day of the week it was
What time it was
What I was doing that morning or later that evening
I cannot remember the day
Only certain moments
As if those moments made up the entirety of that day
The entirety of that phase in my life
These selected memories lead me to wonder about the
moments I'm leaving for my kids

Which moment will make up their day when they remember
Which moment will encompass how they feel towards me
Towards home

These moments seem inconsequential, but they are all
we have of each other
If they are not safe
If they are not open
If they are not filled with more laughter and love than
hurt and pain
What will we search for in life?

Give what you need to be given
What you needed to be given

And know that God will provide for you
And for them
And trust that love is ever present even if our brain
deceives us into forgetting

* * *

Every time something happens, good or bad, every time we as a species increase our capacity for knowledge, for growth, for building, we are simultaneously increasing our individual capacity to receive, to absorb, to acknowledge more within ourselves.

Often times, we're moving too fast. It is in these times that I feel we overlook or underestimate the benefit of obstacles. I think the universe sends us obstacles to slow us down. To nudge us into looking around, to prod us into making sure we've got all we need, we're not skipping any steps, we've mastered what we need to for our next chapter.

* * *

Of the many teachers I've had, one guided me in discovering just how much I can look to little things for learning. He used to encourage us to always stay thirsty for knowledge, to search for knowledge in every person, every interaction, every experience. To be mindful of the divine in the mundane. To look for connections everywhere. He opened me up to the idea that learning happens everywhere. Every moment is a moment meant to bring us closer to ourselves and our Creator. To bring us to Him, not further away from Him. He showed me to look for lessons. In every single thing and every single person. And every mistake and every achievement. In so doing, I learned to really look at my mistakes and my achievements, break them down with a fine-tooth comb. Every failure became just another stepping stone towards my goal: synchrony. He wasn't my first grade teacher or any elementary grade teacher or a teacher in any conventional way we know teachers. But he was truly a guide in every way I can think. God says, *"He who has been given wisdom has been favored."*

Wisdom does not come after our greatest difficulties but in unison with them. In that realization, we can transmute our pain to growth, our tragedy to transformation. In muscle-training, we discover that in order to build stronger muscles, our muscles must first tear. Similarly, our most difficult circumstances can be the ones that build us into stronger, softer, and kinder versions of ourselves, not by not breaking us down but by breaking us open to greater love, greater compassion, giving us a greater capacity to see, give, feel valued, and add value.

* * *

Sister,
You are, and will never cease to be, my better self
You have raised me in ways I cannot explain, ways that travel beyond the reach of words
Ways that lie in truths only God and I know, truths that have inspired life to bind us
I hear your voice singing to the clouds that they may weep, as you have eased my tears
I feel your steady hand guiding that of the wind, as you pushed and pushed me forwards
I see the reflection of your smile in the sun, as you have shared it so selflessly with me
I bask in the beauty of the snow and sand alike, as you have taught me to love all

MOURNING AIR

I shy from the vastness your heart has gifted the sea,
as you have forced me to navigate through it
What I owe to you runs deeper than the waters of the ocean,
along the fluidity of time and bathes in the pools of life itself
For every breath that leaps from my chest, every word
that escapes my lips, every action brought forth
by my hand
Is in your name, sister
You are with me when I close my eyes and your very
presence is what bids them to open

Together we walk, my sister
Forevermore we walk, my sister

—Hamoodi, March 2022
To me, Sara, and Summer

FOURTH BREATH

Perspective

Hamoodi's first semester in college was all online. February 2021 would be his first time going back to live in the U.S. after leaving almost ten years prior, his first time living alone, and his first time on the East Coast. To ease his transition, my dad, my sister, and I accompanied him on that first trip to Boston. We loaded up shopping carts with dorm room essentials from Walmart, stayed up late laughing about failed exams, reminiscing about our own college experiences, Baba reliving every physics exam he struggled with, every street fight, every early morning and late night he'd lived on the same streets just across the river. My dad graduated from Boston University. And here we were, in Cambridge at Maseeh Hall, checking Hamoodi in at MIT. Hamoodi was funny that way; even when he left home, he didn't stray. He talked about the Charles the same way he talked about the Nile.

LEENA MAGDI

> things come back
> we may not know when
> or what the circumstances will be that bring them back
> but we pray they're good ones
> like dropping my brother off at school
> like my dad coming back thirty years later
> things come back
> nothing stays gone
> everything comes full circle

We all fly to California after my master's graduation in Philadelphia. I'm going to a music festival in San Jose, and Hamoodi and my cousin say they'll drop me off. They're going to a concert in San Francisco. It's out of their way, but they say it's fine. On the drive over I tell them about how I failed my DMV renewal test. It's a running joke in the family that I fail these written driving tests. It's always a technical issue: I passed but on the wrong computer, so it didn't count, failed the second time. Hamoodi just got his driver's license. We drive around downtown San Jose a little before they drop me off, exchanging college stories, this time Hamoodi adding in some of his own.

There were so many phases of friendship we were just starting, Habeebi. So many that were only just beginning. So many that'll never come back around.

MOURNING AIR

* * *

Sometimes, when we lose someone we love, grief shocks us into thinking

Oh my God... Why?
How?
How could God?
How could they go?
How could the universe?
How could this happen?

But really...how couldn't they? How couldn't it?
We were determined to leave the day we were determined to come into our life here on earth.

We believe there is injustice in death. I am not talking about the circumstances surrounding death or the causes of death. As they can be particularly unjust. But death itself. We believe death itself to be unjust; that it is an unjust act of God, or the universe, or whichever creed we subscribe to. That it shouldn't happen. Of course, no one says it out loud. It seems like an irrational thing to say. But we do have this unspoken belief that time lasts, that life should last, that we were born to never stop living when the most human thing to do after living is dying. I wonder why. What around us gave us that implausible idea? That any living being continues living? All around us life ends. In Arabic we would call something like this *sunnat al haya* or *the way of life*. That's how I see it, at least. How very Neptunian of us. How very human of us. We have deluded ourselves into expecting life to last. So much so that death makes us angry. But in that anger about death, comes a clarity about life.

The thing about grief is that it changes the way we view things. Every. Thing. Even ourselves. Life, all of a sudden, looks different. But we're the only ones who can see the difference. It's like everything suddenly becomes so clear. But only for us. Only through these grief-stricken glasses. Our relationships change. We change. The way we move through life changes. And we know with certainty that this vision is much clearer than the one we had before. Our perspective shifts. In this way, grief can sometimes be so lonely. But if we listen, in the quiet, in this newfound perspective, peace resides.

> My dad always says to pay attention to things when they're good.
> When you're happy
> What you're doing
> How you're feeling
> How you got there
> What you did to get there
> How you maintained
> What did you change

MOURNING AIR

> Pay attention to all the little details that got you
> to your good place
> Don't just remember the feeling
> Because it'll pass
> And if you weren't paying attention, you'll have a hard
> time getting it back
> Or keeping it a state of being rather than a fleeting
> feeling

* * *

I believe we simultaneously exist within two realms: an outer realm and an inner realm. The outer realm consists of our family, colleagues and co-workers, conditions at work, other people's emotional states, other people's reactions to what we do, the state of affairs in the outside world, our accomplishments and failures, conflict, war and peace. Our boss says something to us we don't like, a friend doesn't invite us out, our partner gives us attitude, we lose a loved one, we lose our homes... We do not control what happens in the outer realm.

Our inner realm, however, is within our control. It consists of our thoughts, beliefs, and emotions. And in turn, it contains the roots from which our behavior and character are formed. The way we present ourselves in the outer realm is directly contingent on the conditions of our inner real; here is where our peace resides. It does not leave these parameters.

The dreams that we have are put in us for a reason: because we can achieve them. Everything we desire, we already are. To achieve, we must first recognize the synchrony that exists within us. In the presence and the absence. In each breath. For every inhale, we must first exhale. In every bus filled with terrified faces, stopped by armed militia, there is an innocent child unafraid to extend his hand, there is a grandmother praying for her and her family's safety, there is a brother carefully watching, distantly guiding. The peace is in the pieces. Each one of us has the capacity to carry that peace with us, even if only in pieces.

* * *

Placing considerable reliance on our external realm conceals the true nature of our peace. It becomes difficult for us to gain peace because we do not have authentic transparency with ourselves. We are unable to reach it. Often times, we look for peace in our outer realm, placing it in the success and stability of external circumstances. We'll say things like *I hope you have a good day today* or *I hope today is a calm day*. We rely on the conditions of our outer realm to satisfy our inner peace. Because sometimes they align, we think, *Yes, when I'm financially stable, I'll have peace* or *When I'm not around certain people, I'll have peace*. And so on. But that is a misconception.

The difficult truth is that it doesn't have to matter whether the kids are calm, whether our work day was hectic, whether we have had a *good* day—we can learn to be the good in each day, the calm for ourselves. Letting outside circumstances dictate our well-being is self-sabotaging. This goes beyond establishing healthy habits like a morning workout or meditation routine or eating healthy. While those factors are necessary, they are not sufficient. This is about rewiring our beliefs, going inwards and seeking our peace, believing that it is a constant state that we hold within us.

* * *

Coming to Egypt made it clear for me that in terms of healing and emotional work, making it to safety was only just the beginning. We lost a lot coming to Egypt. There is no place that is without its own unique set of challenges. However, there is synchrony to be found everywhere, in everything, in every place. Focusing on the good does not dismiss, belittle, or justify the difficult. It does not imply that things should not be rectified. It is a choice of inner peace that will trickle in the little details of our days.

We also gained a lot in coming here. My boys experienced their first summer camp here; my younger sister was able to start college and live at home; there is a favor here that I can either choose to look towards or away from.

LEENA MAGDI

When I learned to pivot, my life changed
learn to pivot
internally
and watch the ripples of change become waves of
transformation

* * *

The other night, I felt grief pushing to resurface, craving an overflow. I could see it in my mind's eye, an ocean of waves confined in a cup. Outside my room, there were some people riding motorcycles. The sound of their tires skidding resembled gunshots. This was not grief. It was terror coming back, surging through my veins. My body remembered. Only, through grief, I've mastered the art of calling my waves in. There was no overflow. There was no resurface. A mere tipping of the cup. Terror is mind numbing. It is petrifying. It is an entity on its own. Much like its close friend, grief.

I could see it. I could smell it. I knew it was familiar. But the thing about terror is that it caused me to doubt myself; I did not trust that I knew what it was. Though I had been there before. Though I knew it intimately, I could not label it, I could not recall it, the terror blinded my memory. Terror is no small enemy. Terror reminds us of the simple truth that is there is very little we control. Once fear takes over, there is little else we can do. It takes an act of continuous physical, psychological, emotional, and spiritual valor to overcome terror. To not allow terror to swallow us, to consume us, our thoughts, our every breath. Once it's in, it's like a thief in the night, it'll steal the rights to everything we own. And let us know it was never ours to begin with. And we will become so helpless, we willfully watch it. It is a skilled parasite feeding off its host. A clever virus with ever-changing faces so we never recognize the real threat; the greatest thing to fear is fear itself.

One of the most paralyzing things about this kind of grief is that once time was no longer faithful, I began to question everything else. Is what I'm feeling intuition? Because I felt dread in the days prior to my brother's death. I knew something horrible was coming. I couldn't sleep at night, imagining what it could be. Now anytime I get an uneasy feeling, I can easily mistake it for something graver. Part of it could be trauma. But part of it could be intuition. I can't discern the difference anymore. In the months leading up to that night in August, I had horrible feelings. Thoughts that kept me up at night. Call it intuition, premonition, whatever you like. I'm not entirely sure what it was.

But I am of the belief that everything in the universe is interconnected, working for us, not against us. And sometimes it gives us little nudges that gift us extra time.

LEENA MAGDI

I often think back to Hamoodi's twenty-first birthday. One of the last memories of all of us together in our house in Garden City, the house my grandfather built in the eighties, making sure each one of his seven kids had a place of their own. When my parents and younger siblings moved back to Sudan, they moved into the apartments on the second floor. My cousin and his family lived in an apartment on the first, and my aunt and her family had always lived on the ground floor. Originally, my uncles and aunts lived in the other apartments, but it was a long time since they'd each left Sudan, so my aunt started renting out their apartments. Since the house was so close to the Iraqi Embassy, Iraqi families coming to Sudan for short bouts of time were regular tenants. Pretty soon, when a lot of Syrian families came to Sudan, the apartments started to stay fuller for longer. That year, there was one Iraqi family and one Tunisian family renting. In a way, that house was a home away from home for many.

Anytime we had a birthday in the house, everyone, from the oldest to the youngest, would get together to cut the cake and sing "Happy Birthday." Hamoodi had recently taken up boxing and wanted to get to his training session. Sara was late as usual and hadn't made it yet, so naturally, we couldn't cut the cake until all members of the family were present. Hamoodi insisted on leaving. Sara was known for running late, and he didn't want to miss his session. *It's just cake*, he said. *It's not a big a deal.* A dreadful knowing tugged at my heart, and I gently squeezed his hand. *Just wait a little longer until Sara and the boys get here, leave after we cut the cake.*

I remember thinking, *He has to stay for this birthday.* It was more of a fearful thought than a loving one. I was worried about something, only, I didn't know what. Yet. He left right after we cut the cake. That was the last birthday we spent together, forty-five days before he was murdered.

* * *

Reframing our imbedded beliefs, even when adopting positive beliefs about ourselves, is a challenge. The reason, I believe, is that there exists an underlying expectation that because we are doing the work, things should start to work out; we shouldn't be triggered. Things should start to align simply because we have started to do the work.

Now that I am getting up earlier and organizing my day, I shouldn't have unexpected issues, after all I am planning for them.

Now that I'm practicing gentle-parenting techniques, I shouldn't have trouble keeping my cool and not losing my temper.

Now that I'm meditating or praying more, I should be less inclined to be angry or irritable.

Now that I'm in a safe place, I won't feel fear; I'll only feel gratitude.

Our expectation is that our problems will decrease once we start working on ourselves, or once we become aware of them. But awareness of the issue is merely the first step; it is not the solution. The reality is the quantity of problems we face is not something we can control, regardless of the habits we put in place. There is an undercurrent of assumptions that if we are trying to do right, things shouldn't go wrong. But they do. What happens in our external realm is independent and exclusive from the inner work we are doing. Our attitude towards our circumstances, towards our self, our self-talk, that voice in our head, the quality of care we give ourselves and others, the pause before action, *that* is the *peace* we can control. Like synchrony, it exists everywhere. Like breath, it is subtle and continuously flowing.

I can still be calm even if nothing in the day was calm.

I can still be okay even if I broke down multiple times today.

I can decide to be good even if today was not a good day.

There exist small mercies in every situation. Making a choice to actively look for them illuminates the wisdom, the synchrony, the peace. Regardless of the circumstance, my job is to look for the small mercy. The little gift. The miracle. Take it and use it to alchemize the rest of the day.

MOURNING AIR

wherever you go, carry your stillness with you...in you

* * *

We all want to be seen, understood, and heard. My body remembers what it felt like every time I was told my English was too American, my laugh was too loud, or my Arabic wasn't Sudanese enough. My questions were too straightforward; my answers were always a little too honest. They weren't cushioned with the soft and subtle nuances familiar to Sudanese cultural discourse. My shoulders started to tense, I started to keep my arms a little closer to my chest, and my breath became a little nervous. There seemed to be something in me that stroked a nerve of discomfort in my surroundings. Or perhaps the discomfort was internal. But all I really wanted was to be understood. And the confusion angered me because I loved the parts of me that were too American. Too California. So I clung to them. I highlighted them even more. When one avenue of expression is muted, the mind finds another. I have always colored my hair blond, it is the color I feel most comfortable in, but in that period of my life, I colored it red.

LEENA MAGDI

The wind has a lot to say today
I wonder if it has ever been told it is too loud
Too pushy
Too windy
I wonder if its need to relieve was ever dismissed or disregarded
I wonder if it knows of other voices belittled
I wonder if it is trying to compensate for every voice silenced

* * *

While I know that being heard, seen, and understood are crucial aspects in any healthy connection, I have learned that to cultivate inner peace, we must stop *searching* for understanding. We must instead start to see ourselves, understand our true essence, and hear ourselves. We must start to speak and live in alignment with our purpose. In so doing, those who do see us will naturally gravitate towards us, and instead of relying on their validation, we will be able to welcome and reciprocate the love. And in the circumstances in which people we love, or life, disappoint us, we will not come undone. The difficult truth of the matter is no one person will ever fully understand anything or everything another has gone through. Each person I have spoken to who left Khartoum had a different story.

MOURNING AIR

The forty-five other people riding on the same bus with us in Arqeen experienced it differently. It is not fair for me to expect anyone else to see things through my eyes, nor can I expect to fully understand anyone else's experience.

The best we can offer one another is presence in love, peace in presence, and grace in the absence of understanding.

> I thank my anger for protecting me when I needed protection
> I thank my bitterness and my resentment for putting me first when I so badly felt abandoned
> I thank my dark places for self-preservation when it mattered
> For demanding the space the rest of me needed to heal
> For giving me no other option but to transform

As time went on, I started to notice how each language brought out different parts of my personality. Initially, I thought I was more *myself* in English. Freer. Louder. Untethered. Less scripted. After all, I told myself, I do *think* in English. But the more time went on, the more I realized it was not that I was less myself in Arabic but rather Arabic allowed me access to areas of myself I hadn't ventured in before. It was new territory for me. It was like I was getting to know different parts of myself in a different language. And that opened me up to opportunities to learn myself, to connect with family, and to understand the culture and community fully, truly, in context.

* * *

How often do we actively show ourselves love? I believe that doing so is a practice in divine love. It gives us the stillness to find the love that exists within us, in all of us, without the need to rely on the external validation of it. When we tap into that divine love, we start to see how it permeates every single thing. With our projects, with our kids, with strangers, with pets. How the universe smiles back at us. For every moment gone wrong, there are so many moments that go right. In every external circumstance, there is an opportunity for inner growth. Through that, we allow ourselves greater capacity to break open, to live the synchrony. To inhale more deeply, purposefully, and exhale slowly, gracefully.

MOURNING AIR

take a moment and think about your greatest love
what made it so great?
was it the other person?
or was it the version of yourself you became when you
came together?
the parts of yourself you discovered?
there are certain people that make it easy for us to be
our true self
that is what we fall in love with
the ease of honest compassion
that is love
that is what love is
the allowing and seeing of true self

when we see ourselves like that
when we become like that
we fall in love
so the trick is
be like that with yourself
don't wait for someone else to bring the best out of you
give your best to the world
and watch how much love comes
be in a state of perpetual self-love

* * *

Accessing our own inner peace transforms us into conduits, allowing us to channel what we've gained from our experiences and then watch the resonance it creates. Tragedy is universal; it is a shared human experience. Everyone experiences it in one way or another.

We must recognize that strength is not something we reach or gain. It is the awareness of our pained vulnerability in every moment and our choice to live each moment wholly. Still.

Peace is the only constant. When we are in our mother's womb, we are encapsulated in peace. When someone dies, we pray for them to rest in peace. Peace is the binding force. The stability. It came with us and resides within us. Realizing this will empower us in ways we cannot comprehend. The anger is inevitable, the grief unsurpassable. But in recognizing our inner peace, the anger can pass through us, and the grief with us, knowing it is merely a part of us, it does not own us. As will the positive emotions, the ecstasy, the joy, the ups and the downs, they are part of our journey; they are not the journey. They do not control us. All that remains is peace. Peace is in the soul. It is an entity all on its own. We came from peace and we will return to peace. It is soft and subtle stillness.

This understanding will unintentionally transfer to how we deal with others. Peace goes hand in hand with kindness, creating more peace, kindness with oneself, kindness with one's family, kindness in interpersonal and intrapersonal relationships. Peace is quiet, but it is contagious. It is a powerful voice for those brave enough to give rise to it.

* * *

I've learned that we must humble ourselves
If we don't, life will
I've learned that everyone in our life, every one,
will hurt us
Sometimes the hurt is unwarranted and inexcusable
But that's life
And that's people
And we must forgive
Because that's life
And it's okay
I've learned that to be happy we must actively make a
choice every day
We must love God
I've learned that God is in everything
He is ever present
In ways we cannot begin to comprehend
And His mercy, His mercy...
We owe everything to His mercy

LEENA MAGDI

We belong to Him and unto Him we shall return
Love God and everything else falls into place
I've learned that God is in everything and family is the most important thing
And that, by far, is the best lesson

* * *

In the experience of grief, we perhaps unintentionally validate the joy we once had with our loved one; the love we shared. We cannot have one without the other. Awareness of this synchrony in life is transformative. I like to think of pain and peace like two hands belonging to the same entity and awareness of the synchrony in life as the space that binds their interlock.

What do peace and love have in common?

They are little bits of stillness in a world filled with impermanence.

In that, there is permanence, both scattered in fleeting moments, never in one place for too long but in every place for a little while.

MOURNING AIR

In every interaction and situation
There exists a piece for us
Peace to be discovered within us
Sometimes in the form of a lesson to be learned
Or taught
Sometimes a joy to be had
Sometimes delivered through a specific person
Sometimes it's for us to find and sometimes it's for us to wait for
Either way
There always exists a missing or should I say hidden piece to the puzzle
Sometimes these pieces tend to overlap
When they do
When you notice that your positive events are bringing up the same piece across different categories of your life
Hold on to that piece
Hold on to that peace
To that lesson
To that person
That is love
When that person is sharing with you across domains of your life
They are a hidden piece of love
Peace in love
Recognize and appreciate that piece in them

The peace in them
Make them a permanent part of your life
Appreciate the gift-Giver by recognizing His gifts
They are scattered everywhere
In every place and every person
Within
Love is when those pieces overlap across the board
Love is in peace

FIFTH BREATH

Hope

The first few times we are faced with challenges or difficult situations, we have energy, we have stamina.
We mistake that for hope.
That is not hope.
Hope arises out of desperation. It is the only positive emotion that comes during, and, or, with negative events.
We learn how to be hopeful. It is a cognitive process.
It is not a feeling.
It is a knowing.

* * *

We measure life by time. But I feel we do ourselves and the ones we love a disservice in doing so. What if, instead, we measured life through the impact we left on others?

In Khartoum, many people make a living out of selling things on the street. Some sell fruit; others sell clothes, jewelry, kids' toys, you name it. These transactions are usually fairly quick as the sellers must make their way off the street as soon as the traffic lights turn. In addition to those who are trying to make an honest living, there are others who violently rob vehicles stopped at traffic lights; they are known to target young people and women. And characteristic of cities with large income disparities between the rich and the poor, many others are forced to beg for money on the street. On the streets with stop lights that work, when the light turns red, the gaps between, behind, and in front of every car are flooded with people—each person with their own story.

A couple of weeks before my brother passed, he bought prayer beads from a young man on the street. Hamoodi didn't have enough cash to pay him on the spot, so he asked the young man if he'd be willing to get in the car with him to go down the street to his friend's house and get the rest of the money. The young man agreed, and with all his merchandise, in ninety seconds—the time it takes for the light to turn—got in the car. Hamoodi's friend didn't have enough cash, so Hamoodi, his friend, and the young man selling beads drove around from friend to friend, cousin to cousin, until my brother collected the full amount and paid him. He then dropped him back off at his everyday spot.

* * *

MOURNING AIR

If they ever tell my story, let them say I bled openly
That my heart's influence was boundless; it's light, at times,
dimmed but never silenced.
Let them speak of my love in all its lionheartedness
For if nothing else
That is what I offer this world
My actions will not echo across the centuries
My name will be lost to memory
But the love I share will live endlessly.
And if they mention nothing at all
Let them say my love was immortal
Its reach blind, embrace kind, touch gentle;
Let them say my heart danced with the wind
And that my mind followed, cautious
Afraid of tragedy but fully aware
Of the strength to be found in calamity

—Hamoodi

* * *

Dignity. My brother treated everyone with dignity. The days of his funeral, our house was filled with love. From family and friends but also from strangers. From people living on the street. People he'd helped in one way or another. People he spent quality time with. When I say he was generous, I do not mean materialistically, although he was, but more so, he was generous with his love. He offered space for grace to people from all walks of life. He understood the secret of synchrony in life. That pain and peace coexist. That for deep trust, we must remain in constant risk of betrayal. That to experience a love that surpasses time, we must give indiscriminately.

My brother exuded sublime kindness. He treated everyone as if he knew with conviction their intentions were honest. His kindness extended beyond his close circle, to those who held the greatest risk of betrayal, to those who couldn't possibly reciprocate it, to those who could potentially harm him. It was as if he knew his time was short. Or perhaps that time, in general, is short. The more time we've had, the less time we have.

* * *

Two months after his passing, with faculty support, his friends in Boston organized a three-day memorial service for him on the MIT campus. It was carefully, lovingly, and so thoughtfully put together. There was space for everyone to share their stories and their loss. Everyone had space. Regardless of the amount of time they spent with him. What was being shared or implied was that this loss belongs to all of us. He belongs to all of us and we will all hold this together.

MOURNING AIR

Baba wore a fancy suit
the kind you'd love to steal from him
Mama wore a beautiful dress with a flowy cardigan that
complemented it
we walked around your campus
saw the different classrooms and buildings
passed by your freshman dorms
the sun set blue and orange
the speeches were moving
but you had already moved on
and all I kept thinking to myself was we shouldn't be here
all of us shouldn't be here together
not today

this is what I imagined we'd be doing for your
graduation day
with you leading our way
and instead of black we'd all be wearing red
to match your tie
but fate doesn't work like that, I guess

we are too early

your memorial was beautiful
overflowing with love, just like you

* * *

From an impact lens, there was nothing short about Hamoodi's life. Is this a tragedy? The worst. Is his life defined by it? Absolutely not. His life was far greater. And yes, we can sit and wonder about what he could have and would have been doing and what was taken from him.

But that, in my opinion, would not be speaking justice to his life in the way that he deserves. Because there is so much he did do. So much he did give. So much that could never be taken from him. Even through this tragedy. People get to live to eighty or ninety years and do not reach the level of completion that he reached.

* * *

In death, we can no longer give; however, in Islam, the concept of Sadaqah Jariyah permits the living to give to the dead through acts of charity in their name. My brother was generous with all he had. Hours before he was killed, he gave all the money he had in his wallet to children on the street selling gum. A Sadaqah Jariyah is a continuous charity, an act of kindness or service done with the hope that its reach transcends this world and continues to multiply after one passes. It can be knowledge shared, trees planted, anything that reciprocates, gifts that grow. Water that runs deep, trees that grow tall. It is a common practice in our community to start a Sadaqah Jariyah for a loved one after they pass. My brother's generosity became apparent after he passed in all of the services started to honor his name.

One of the initiatives formed in his name was repairing four water wells that served a community on the outskirts of Khartoum. My mother worked for an NGO that served a specific community for years. They did not have access to running water or electricity. One of the NGO's main goals was to establish running water to families and schools. Hamoodi's friends organized and collected donations to repair water wells and build solar panels to power the wells so that they are not bound to rely on electricity that is rarely, if ever, available. After the war started, we were told that it was these solar-powered wells that became the source of sustenance for these communities and their neighboring communities during the war.

Another form of Sadaqah Jariyah that is ongoing is the Mohamed Magdi Taha Memorial Scholarship Fund created by the family and a few of Hamoodi's friends to honor his legacy of helping others and the community. Our aim with the scholarship is to support students who want to study STEM and/or the arts (two things Hamoodi loved and was studying at MIT) in the U.S. The scholarship focuses on empowering students to tap into their inner upstander—a quality Hamoodi personified.

LEENA MAGDI

The love people poured into keeping my brother's name alive after he was gone is a testament to everything he gave in his life.

>when I hear the saying *love guides all*
>I rarely think it is referring to love the emotion
>or the feeling of love
>because that is a thing fleeting
>I rather think about the action of love
>that regardless of how I may feel
>I value you
>I will honor you
>I will hold you dear
>because of who you are and who I am
>not because of something as temporary and fickle as a feeling

* * *

There is something to be said about loss and what it does in bringing people together. People need people. We now have a stronger closeness to the people who loved Hamoodi, to his friends. *Ana ma 3ndi akho laken akhwani kotar. I don't have a brother, but my brothers are many.* That was something Hamoodi used to say. The way his friends have shown up in our lives really speaks to the type of people they are and the type of person he was. There's this familiar closeness now between us because of our shared loss. That whatever you need, call me, I'll be there. And they are. And we are. It's almost like a blood bond. Maybe it's Hamoodi facilitating things from wherever he is, if souls can do things like that. I like to think they do.

The only people I feel comfortable talking about Hamoodi with—without it resulting in a solemn change of tone, averted eyes, awkward silences, or nervous chatter—are his friends. Sometimes we will talk about him like he's still here; sometimes we'll acknowledge he's gone. Either way, it's always okay. We'll talk about the funny things he used to do, an annoying thing he said, anything and everything, and it won't even have to be the main topic of the conversation. There's an ease and understanding in connection with them, even those we met after his death.

In his passing, we have inherited his company. I see him in them. There are some friends that we have known for years in his life, others we met after the fact at his memorial, and others at the hospital by his body. But the feeling of closeness, of knowing, transferred almost immediately. We all have friends that we can go months, sometimes years, without speaking to and then come back and it will be as if no time has passed. That is how it's been with Hamoodi's friends. It's like they have always been this close to me. Their names have always been in my most recent WhatsApp chats. They have always been there. In getting to know them in this new way now, I also feel like I have a different knowing of my brother. Through their eyes. It is an interesting experience getting to know someone from different angles after they're gone.

My brother's friends carry me. They've carried my sisters. They've carried my parents.

* * *

MOURNING AIR

I have this theory
to treat love like a person
we say love alone isn't enough
and that becomes enough reason for us to leave
but why leave love alone?
If we know it is not enough?
why leave it to fend for itself?
why not support our love like we support our closest ties?
with kindness, grace, understanding and support
so the object of our love understands that it is love that is
communicating
so that there is space for mistakes and misunderstandings
so that there is space for the depth that comes with
distance and pain
may we learn to love deeply and lightly
may we learn to see beyond the many ways our egos
manifest and fool us
may we learn to see the depths always
all ways

* * *

Hamoodi was my little brother, but he was so big to me. He is so big to me. I looked up to him so much. I still do. He gave abundantly, effortlessly, and quietly. I always knew he was generous, but I didn't know to what extent. A close friend, very dear to my heart, had this to say about my brother:

"Hamoodi had no walls. Everyone can get in his car. Everyone can get his love. And so yes. Everyone is in deep mourning. He was such a sweet judge of character." —Jerrie

Time leaves space for perceived injustice. Those who die young do not have the same opportunities as those who live a long life simply because their time is shorter. Impact, however, is impartial to time. When it comes to impact, even the baby who died in infancy has left a significant impact on their parents. Even an unborn baby has impacted the womb that carried him or her. Anything, anyone, that was has left a trace, has impacted something, someone.

That, to me, is worthwhile, worth something. That isn't to say any impact is a positive one. But once we internalize this concept, we can start to frame our lives around the impact we would like to impart. Our role becomes to try, as best we can, to ensure the time we have is spent adding value to ourselves and those around us. Understanding the truth of synchrony in life allows us to look beyond temporary circumstances and see the shared humanity in all of us.

MOURNING AIR

* * *

War and sudden loss make it difficult to walk through life without fear. But I've come to see that when fear shows its face, the best way to pass through it is through submission to something greater. To the Creator. To the universe. To our shared humanity. With an interconnected sense of hope and faith. Hope that I have what it takes to get myself out. And faith that if I cannot, if indeed there is nothing I can do, then whatever happens is for the best. Is for my good. Even if it seems like the worst. Even in death, goodness can be found. When my time comes, I have to believe that everything good I have to give I have given. Everything good I have to receive I have received. And if my time has come, then in this world there exists no good left for me to receive and no good left for me to give. I have given all that is good for me to give and taken all that is good for me to take.

Letting go is not the same as being helpless. Fear will fool us into believing that they are the same. That letting go is defeat. This is where the inner work of peace comes in. When faith and hope work together. In times when we cannot do anything to change our external circumstances, we can still master our outlook, our inner peace, and remain hopeful. Hold that little bit of control. When we do not succumb to the fear, we cannot be consumed by it. We can let go in faith that external circumstances will continue to change and eventually align, and in any situation our strengths will nourish us. So that when the storm passes, we emerge a powerful, transformed version of ourselves.

* * *

It took us about a week to cross the border into Egypt. After my grandmother passed away at the border crossing in Arqeen, we took her back to the nearest city, where we had family, in order to bury her. Dongola was four hours away. We spent one night in Dongola and left the next morning for the other border crossing, Halfa. Within one year, my father had buried his only son and his mother. We had already lost so much. And it felt like in leaving, we were losing it all again.

>
> I know we're all travelers
> and this here is just one stop
> and though blood is but a worldly bind
> I'm so glad we are bound by it
> for me it is extra assurance that I will surely find you
> again
> you will be my signpost
> I'm so glad God let us have you
> I'm so glad I got to hold you
> I'm so glad I got to be a close observer in your journey
> I'm so glad for all the times you held me

MOURNING AIR

As April came to an end, we finally crossed the border and spent some time in Aswan, Egypt, before making the trip to Cairo. I remember that first night, relief slowly making its way through my body as I sank into the pillow. Drifting into sleep, my mind took me back to the brown leather couch in our living room in Garden City. I can't recall exactly what it was I was doing back then, maybe a project or essay for my master's program. It was Hamoodi's first winter break from college. *Lon,* his favorite nickname for me, *why don't you post your work anymore? I miss your writing. Just keep at it.* I had a small writing page on Instagram, something I created a year or so prior to share my writing with the hopes of one day putting together a book.

* * *

I haven't known hope to be grand gestures of strength. Maybe sometimes it can be. But mainly I have heard hope in whispers of encouragement. My mother wanting to pray by Hamoodi's body in the hospital. I've seen hope in my sons and nephews and their ability to run around and play and sing on the bus, even when hungry, and tired, and thirsty. I've watched hope crawl around my father's grief-stricken face as he led us from one border crossing to another until we were finally safe.

LEENA MAGDI

When there is no more inspiration, no awe, no want or desire to continue, hope is there and it doesn't just sustain, it transforms. When everything else has left and we want to give up, hope comes in and says, *I'm here, keep going, we can do it, we are not going to stop.*

* * *

I've made a bed out of your things
In your city
Walking the streets, you used to walk
Talking to all the people you used to talk to
Hoping to catch a little bit of you
I've made a nest out of your people
And they've nestled me warm
But when I'm alone
I open up the suitcase that I arranged
Of all of the things you left behind
And I curl up inside it and sleep for a little bit
That is where I've found the most peace

AFTERWORD

I don't believe grief happens in stages. My experience has been a kaleidoscope of many stages in synchrony. The first days after Hamoodi was killed, I was shocked, broken, and confused. But I also felt an overwhelming surge of acceptance. I remember the most repeated thought in my mind was *I accept this, God. I accept what you've written.* I felt connected with the divine, with His will. I felt a connection with the unseen.

But that feeling didn't last. I think it was a gift to get me through the shock. Now it comes and goes sporadically.

Denial started to creep in months later in random moments: driving to work, hearing a familiar song, in mid-conversation. It was a wave of anxiety, sadness, and disbelief. *But so much has happened. How is it that I haven't spoken to you? It can't be. It doesn't make sense. I don't understand.*

Those moments didn't last either. They, too, now come and go sporadically.

I realized that grief is a mosaic of stages occurring in synchrony all with equal importance and impact.

What happens when the worst happens is that we lose our sense of self for a little while. At least, that's been my experience. Discovering my own character strengths became another window to actuating the code to my inner restoration, my growth, my breaking-open. Character strengths are really about self-awareness.

The helpful bit that comes with knowing what our innate strengths are is that we are then able to just look for them. They provide solace in the knowledge that even when I'm devastated, I'm still okay. I'm okay because I have this inner set of strengths that get to work. Without my conscious effort. We can look for the ways they are showing up. Like helpful hands. So anytime I noticed I was listening to a lot of spiritual podcasts or reading books about loss, I realized these are my strengths pushing me forward. Keeping me afloat. Like breath. We don't have to think about it most of the time. We do not actually have to do anything because our strengths work for us during our times of great difficulty and great joy. We do not need to actively activate them. When we are in the midst of tragedy, in the middle of the wave, when we haven't realized we can keep breathing, it's a great relief to know that helpful hands exist.

But once we are aware of our breath, we can start taking mindful breaths. Practicing breathwork. Our signature strengths are the same. They are a special form of self-awareness. Knowing myself, knowing what I have to give, keeps me from feeling helpless and hopeless. So I started to think, how far can I go if I start using them intentionally?

My strengths connected me to the power that was created for me and in me, the power that exists in each person uniquely coded to their journeys and lives. While some connections between my grieving and healing processes and my signature strengths are straightforward, like changes in perspective that can come from losing a loved one, others, like honesty, are subtle. My goal with this book is not to tell you how to define each strength; I believe we all have different ways of expressing the same strength, and we can look at the same scenario and see the same strength illustrated in different ways or perhaps see an entirely different strength. I only wish to share the profound ways they have enabled me to live in synchrony with my grief. Like life's breath, they are with us during our most joyous times as well as our most trying times. Awareness of our strengths gives us the ability to nourish and cultivate them. In so doing, we empower ourselves with tools within us that alleviate our pain and enhance our peace. For anyone interested in discovering their own innate strengths and starting to see how their strengths have been working for them, the VIA

LEENA MAGDI

Character Strengths Survey is simple, straightforward, and life-changing: https://viacharacter.org.

What has changed for me in my grief, and through my own strengths, is my ability to welcome each stage and feeling without judgment. I don't feel guilty for the moments of denial; I don't feel like I've turned my back on Hamoodi for the moments of acceptance. I don't feel ungrateful for the moments of anger. I have learned to breathe through every feeling. To feel it, fully, wherever it may land in my body. Sometimes it's a block in my throat, sometimes it's a sinking feeling in my stomach, sometimes it's extra sensitivity in my skin where I can feel the air change. Whatever form it decides to greet me with, I have learned to accept every feeling, always, in all ways.

I am always in a state of grieving my brother. Loss is not something we have been accustomed to accepting. One minute we're talking, laughing, arguing with our loved one, and the next, they're gone. We can spend years building a home, pouring ourselves into it, and be forced to leave and leave everything behind. When it is sudden, when there is an injustice involved, acceptance can feel wrong. But what I have learned is that accepting something happened is not the same as excusing it. It is not a release of grief. It is simply a release. A longer breath.

MOURNING AIR

That's the thing about grief. It may change form, like love, it may look different and feel different throughout different phases of our life and with different people and things, but it is always there, like breath.

Healing happens every day, in our everyday things. It's not a huge epiphany one day, or enough time to pass, or the right person to say the right things. It is quiet awareness that we are capable of being. It's in our breath. We keep breathing even when devastated. It's a turn of the head towards what continues to grow. It's paying attention to our breath. It's paying attention to our strengths. It's learning to be intentional.

Healing is also an acknowledgment of the bigger picture. That death is not loss. And we are all going to die one day. It is a pledge to add value while we still can.

Most importantly, healing does not erase the grief. It doesn't make it lighter. It doesn't make it easier. Grief is never done. Neither is love. In their experience exists a distinct heartbeat that will undoubtedly permeate into every aspect of our lives. Healing only allows us to use it to push forwards. It gives us a healthy way to live with grief.

The air may be different, but we are still breathing.

Arqeen border crossing.
Pictures taken by my then five-year-old son,
April 26, 2023.

Same pictures, edited by my then five-year-old son while waiting at the border crossing, April 26, 2023.

www.ingramcontent.com/pod-product-compliance
Lightning Source LLC
LaVergne TN
LVHW061532070526
838199LV00034B/639/J